Currier and Ives

THE IRISH AND AMERICA

Currier and Ives
THE IRISH AND AMERICA

Kevin O'Rourke

HARRY N. ABRAMS, INC., PUBLISHERS

Dedication

To the O'Dwymans

Some years ago, my wife, whose name is Kathleen Dwyer, and I were at the beach on the north shore of Long Island with our four young children. My two, Brian and Karen O'Rourke, and her two, Jason and Jennifer Norman, had built a sand and driftwood residence that they named "The O'Dwyman Castle" by combining all the names into one. It was a happy moment to remember and so I dedicate this book to "The O'Dwymans."

Acknowledgments

Thank you Brother Charles B. Quinn for making available the research facilities of the Irish Collection at Iona College Library, New Rochelle, New York. Thank you Diane Ranno and Cheryl Milde for typing the manuscript. Thank you Terry Rourke, my brother from San Francisco, for your incisive suggestions and comments. And thanks to my editor, Robert Morton of Harry N. Abrams, who made it all happen.

EDITORIAL NOTE:
Except as otherwise indicated, all the prints reproduced in this book are from the author's collection.

PAGE 2:
A detail of *"Auld Times" at Donnybrook Fair.* (See page 55)

EDITOR:
Robert Morton

DESIGNER:
Maria Learmonth Miller

LIBRARY OF CONGRESS CATALOGING-IN-PUBLICATION DATA

O'Rourke, Kevin.
Currier and Ives : the Irish and America / Kevin O'Rourke.
p.   cm.
Includes bibliographical references.
ISBN 0-8109-4036-1
1. Currier & Ives—Catalogs. 2. Ireland in art—Catalogs.
3. Irish in art—Catalogs. 4. Irish Americans in art—Catalogs.
I. Title.
NE2312.C8A4   1995
769.92—dc20
                                                            95-1154

Published in 1995 by Harry N. Abrams, Incorporated, New York
A Times Mirror Company

Printed and bound in
Hong Kong

Contents

THE VILLAGE OF ROSTREVOR

Currier and Ives
A BRIEF HISTORY

In 1835 Nathaniel Currier, an artist and engraver, established N. Currier's Press at 1 Wall Street in New York City. Currier prepared sheet music for reproduction, made commercial illustrations, and, like many other artists and engravers of the times, struggled to make a living. He worked largely unnoticed for about five years until a major catastrophe, which destroyed the lives of many people, transformed him from being an unknown artist to a figure of national renown.

On January 13, 1840, a popular modern steamboat called *The Lexington* burned and sank in Long Island Sound. Events like this were usually reported in a strictly narrative form in the newspapers of the day, but an enterprising New York paper, the *Sun,* decided to publish a supplement to give a fuller account of the tragedy. The editor commissioned young Nathaniel Currier to make an engraving of the event that could be printed on a separate sheet and inserted in the supplement. Currier pictured the steamboat engulfed in flames and sinking, with people clamoring aboard life rafts while others floundered helplessly in the water. At first the pictures were in black ink only, but after a few days Nathaniel had set up an assembly line so that each print could be colored by hand. Eventually, thousands of hand-colored prints found their way to an eager audience. The public had never seen such a dramatic event rendered so realistically in color. The presses and colorists worked day and night to supply the demand. Copies of the supplement were distributed nationally and Currier gained wide recognition. The success of his own business was virtually assured.

Recognizing the appeal of color prints of popular subjects, which people used on their walls as decorations, Currier thereafter mostly geared his business to making and selling such prints. Prints sized ten by fourteen inches sold at twenty-five cents, larger ones, seventeen by twenty-six inches, sold for three dollars, not an insubstantial sum at the time.

Business was brisk, and in 1852 Currier hired James Merrit Ives as his bookkeeper. Ives was an artist in his own right, but he had an excellent business mind and within a few years he was made a full partner. In 1866 Currier and Ives established their factory at 33 Spruce Street to turn out pictures. Currier had previously opened a retail shop at 152 Nassau Street; the firm later moved to 125, 123, and 115 Nassau Street.

The technique that Currier and Ives used for their prints was lithography, a way of multiplying images that had been devised only a half century before. Simply put, the process is based on the fact that water and oil do not mix. First, an image is drawn on stone, usually limestone, most of which came originally from Solnhofen in Bavaria. Properly cut and ground smooth, this stone offers a surface that is almost totally free of grain or texture. Using greasy crayons, an artist draws the image directly on the stone. Water is washed over the surface of the stone, coating everything except the areas where the greasy crayon has been. When ink with an oily base is rolled onto the stone it adheres only to the areas containing the drawing, since water rejects the oily ink elsewhere. Paper is then pressed onto the stone and the inky image is thus transferred. With fresh applications of ink to the stone, the image may be printed almost indefinitely. At Currier and Ives, each printing stone was kept so that future demand for prints could be met. If no need was found for a stone, its surface could be scrubbed and a new lithograph could be drawn upon it.

Although differently colored inks may be printed one at a time in lithography, the Currier and Ives color prints were made from a basic black and white image that was then colored by hand. One of the artists colored a master print. As other prints came off the stone, this master print served as a model for a team of less-skilled colorists, which, in the case of Currier and Ives, consisted of some twelve teenage girls. Working assembly-line style, the girls each applied one color, passing the print down the line until a complete, fully colored version was ready.

Some of the well-known artists who worked for Currier and Ives included Arthur Fitzwilliam Tate, George Henry Durrie, and James E. Butterworth. The firm also had its own staff of artists, some of whom became famous in their own right, including Fanny Palmer, Louis Maurer, Charles Parsons, and Thomas Worth. Most Currier and Ives prints, however, were the combined efforts of several artists.

The firm usually reserved its best illustrators for the larger prints, and the names of those artists appeared on the base of the print along with the title or subject description. The majority of Currier and Ives's smaller prints, however, list no artist along with the title: it was common at that time for engravers to copy from each

O'SULLIVAN'S CASCADE–LAKE OF KILLARNEY

other. Currier and Ives were no exception; many of their small folio prints, including a good number of the Irish views, were copied from an English engraver named Bartlett.

For the most part, we don't really know the artists who worked on the Currier and Ives Irish-American prints. They were most likely staff people, who based their versions on old black and white engravings by other artists or, in some cases, on photographs, or even engraved illustrations from newspapers or magazines. Reworking these sources, the artists made them into the colorful images that Currier and Ives then copyrighted.

Currier and Ives was only one of many companies of the era that made a business by employing artists to draw on stone, but they were the most successful. Their production of prints was enormous—some seven thousand subjects—and the firm remained in business for seventy-five years, throughout the middle and latter part of the nineteenth century.

In addition to selling prints in their own shop, Currier and Ives sold wholesale to peddlers, who traveled the city hawking prints to whomever they could. Their audience was largely of working people, who could only afford cheap prints. To suit a broad, popular taste, the prints chronicled all aspects of American life, from the growth in the cities to the beautiful countryside. Other popular subjects were the westward expansion, the life of the Indian, the era of the clipper ships, and the drama of

steam on the rails and at sea. Currier and Ives prints also documented America's historical past and all the hobbies and sports of the time, including hunting, fishing, boxing, and horse racing. Others showed pretty girls, children, and fruit and flower still lifes.

Like most East Coast cities, New York in the late nineteenth century saw a large influx of people from Ireland. To attract these immigrants, many of them quite understandably homesick, the Currier and Ives offerings also included many nostalgic views of the Old Country.

Currier and Ives both became well-known personalities of the city, and both lived to a ripe old age. Currier died of heart disease in 1888, and Ives hung on until 1895, when the business was transferred to the sons of the founders, Ed Currier and Chauncey Ives. Not having the same vision or business acumen of their fathers, the sons eventually split up; Ed sold out to Chauncey in 1902, and the firm went out of business for good in 1907. At the time, approximately four thousand of the old lithographic stones were destroyed.

The work of Nathaniel Currier and James Merrit Ives is documented in many books. The emphasis there, quite naturally, is on the large collection of Americana pictures. But within the body of Currier and Ives work are the examples reproduced in this book, many of them seldom reproduced elsewhere. They document an important part of the Irish-American immigrant experience and heritage in the United States.

INTRODUCTION

The work of Currier and Ives in documenting the history of the United States from 1840 to 1907 is well known. Their beautiful prints portrayed America in all its glory: New England country scenes, great Clipper ships, Mississippi River steamboats, fire engines, horse racing, Native American life, and the Old West. These prints have become collector's items: many of them are valued at over $10,000, depending on the quality of the example, the subject matter, and its rarity.

Less well known is the fact that Currier and Ives also created a large body of work that celebrated the arrival in America of millions of Irish, most of whom were fleeing the Great Famine and its aftermath. The firm made more than two hundred prints dealing with explicitly Irish subjects. These included the leaders of the Fenian party, the important early Catholic bishops, and great leaders and revolutionaries in Ireland, such as Daniel O'Connell, Charles Stewart Parnell, and Robert Emmet. They pictured as well a vast array of beautiful scenes from all over Ireland, including the Giant's Causeway, the Meeting of the Waters in County Wicklow, the popular Lakes of Killarney, and the Shores of Connemara. Other prints captured great historical moments in Irish history such as the Siege of Limerick and the Battle of the Boyne. Still others showed how the people lived and dressed, and how they enjoyed themselves.

As well as portraying the beauty of the old country in more than fifty different views, the prints document the history of the Irish from ancient times through the last half of the nineteenth century. They emphasize the good times more than the bad, and the victories more than the defeats of the Irish people.

From the earliest days to the end of their printing business, Currier and Ives never issued any prints derogatory to the Irish. Other media of the day, *Harper's Weekly* magazine, for example, and the New York newspapers that ran the cartoons of Thomas Nast, often showed the Irish negatively, as ill-educated and crude. Currier and Ives, on the other hand, paid respectful attention to their achievements in America and in the old country. Some journals, for example, depicted the Fenians as a movement that hurt Ireland's interest. Fenian leaders were portrayed as "dynamiters," much as today's media labels Irish Republican Army activists as terrorists. In the world of Currier and Ives, however, Thomas Francis Meagher and William Smith O'Brien were shown as "Ireland's patriots of 1848," although they had attacked police stations in the course of their demonstrations. Daniel O'Connell was

"The Great Liberator," Charles Stewart Parnell was "The Great Land Agitator," and Robert Emmet, who led a brief rebellion that resulted in the assassination of the Lord Lieutenant of Ireland, was "Ireland's martyr of freedom." These men were accorded the same dignity as American notables of the day such as Presidents Polk, Lincoln, or Garfield.

This was not mere pandering to an audience on the part of Currier and Ives. Many of the patriots of the Irish cause, such as Thomas Francis Meagher, had careers on this side of the Atlantic and many fought on the side of freedom here. Currier and Ives glorified their achievements in the New World, showing "Fighting Irish" Generals Corcoran, Mulligan, and Meagher leading Irish brigades in the Civil War as well as the construction of the imposing Saint Patrick's Cathedral in New York City.

Many authors have written about the successful transformation of the Irish immigrants who went on to achieve success in different aspects of American life. What the Currier and Ives prints clearly show is that this vast immigrant population was fired by ideals of revolution, patriotism, and an unyielding sense of justice. With all this, they retained love and concern for their old country.

Some four million Irish, considering themselves exiles from their native land, came to these shores during the era of Currier and Ives—the latter part of the nineteenth century. Their descendants today have grown to some forty-four million people, most of whom have become completely assimilated into American culture. Alas, most have little knowledge of the early struggles in this country of their Irish ancestors. Currier and Ives, for their own reasons, helped to create a positive documentation of this chapter in the history of their people.

As the great wave of Irish immigration declined in the 1890s, Currier and Ives was also declining, due to changing tastes and advances in photography. The demand for their prints receded, and the firm went out of business in 1907. The era of cheap, decorative color images especially designed for the walls of the average person's home was over.

For preserving knowledge of their heroes, acquaintance with their home landscape, and pride in their heritage, Irish-Americans owe a debt of gratitude to Currier and Ives. The best way to repay it may be to preserve and appreciate these fine old prints. Some may wish to collect them. At the very least it can be said that Currier and Ives show Irish-Americans in living color who they are and where they came from.

THE LAND OF IRELAND

Irish-Americans have often seemed to believe that once upon a time they were a noble people who lived in a fairy-tale country. Currier and Ives reinforced this fantasy by selling them images of Ireland that showed a land of verdant valleys, magical mountains, and lyrical winding rivers against a backdrop of beautiful natural wonders. Everywhere in these prints there are remains, in various states of repair, of evidence that these enchanted people lived in mansions and castles both large and small.

Some of these images, *The Gap of Dunloe* and *Beauties of Irish Scenery,* for example, are clearly fanciful visions of reality, designed to enhance the myth. Others, such as *Lismore Castle, The Valley of the Blackwater,* and *Rapids of Doonass,* are more realistic views. Bridging the two forms is the print entitled *A Scene in Old Ireland,* which conveys an eerie landscape that is nevertheless inhabited by perfectly real people. Curiously, in the view of *The Giant's Causeway,* the fanciful vision of the Currier and Ives print is less astonishing than the sensations one actually has standing before this remarkable geological formation.

Physically, Ireland is shaped like a saucer, flat in the interior and surrounded by mountains all along the coastline. The famine of the 1840s devastated the local economies of the people who lived in the mountains of the west and south. The resulting depopulation of those counties, as well as other rural areas of Ireland, had the long-term effect of keeping large parts of them almost like national parks, undisturbed by development. They were never designated for preservation as such, but have nonetheless been set aside as if in a time warp for the present generation to enjoy. They remain for the people who left them to go back and visit, whether they are from Australia, Argentina, Canada, or the United States.

Today these mountains are full of the remains of tiny abandoned stone villages, where, in Currier and Ives times, access was by horseback along a river path or stream that wound its way up the valleys. Much of this marginal land, unsuitable or unprofitable for farming, has fallen into the hands of the forestry service, which is rapidly transforming the moors and heather of Ireland into evergreen forests that are being harvested for jobs and cash.

Many of the castles are preserved for visitation by the public. Some have been turned into conference centers or hotels catering to the affluent overseas tourist. Some are abandoned as beyond hope of salvaging or restoration. Other properties—castles, mansions, and even modest farmhouses—have been sold to Europeans and North Americans as holiday and retirement homes. In Currier and Ives's time, however, the mansions and castles were the private residences of an aristocratic landlord class, whose forebears had received large tracts of land as rewards for participating in one of the numerous English invasions of Ireland. Families of the original owners still lived on the land, but were reduced to being tenants, farming plots that were rarely more than an acre or two. This situation gave rise to a continuously unstable political situation, an aspect of Irish history that will be told in subsequent chapters of this book.

Opposite top:
THE GAP OF DUNLOE

Opposite bottom:
ROSS CASTLE—LAKE OF KILLARNEY

The Giant's Causeway—County Antrim

These stone columns are the remains of a bridge built sixty million years ago by an Irish giant called Finn McCool to connect Ireland with Scotland. The bridge enabled Finn to cross the North Channel and subdue the occasional challenges he faced from the residents of the Scottish Highlands. All that remains are the bridge's upright columns of support covering three acres in County Antrim and a smaller area on Staffa Island off the Scottish coast.

The work of Finn McCool in carving these prismatic forms rivals any pyramid in the desert. Yet there are those who claim that these forty thousand hexagonal columns were not chiseled out of rock and set down here as the foundation of a road, but were some magical result of cooling lava from an ancient volcano. A volcano in Ireland? Really! Next thing they would have us believe is that the warmth of the Gulf Stream could even grow palm trees on this North Atlantic island. A thoughtful visitor to this place will stop and look at the clustered columns, so neatly arranged and fitted together, and will ask himself:

> With skill so like, yet so surpassing art,
> With such design, so just in every part,
> That reason pauses, doubtful if it stand
> The work of mortal, or immortal hand.

LISMORE CASTLE—COUNTY WATERFORD

Situated on the bank of the Blackwater River, not far from the southern port of Youghal, Lismore Castle was built originally by King John, son of Henry II, for its strategic importance. For a while it was the home of Sir Walter Raleigh. In 1589, he sold it to an English adventurer named Richard Boyle, who received the English title of Earl of Cork, and whose descendants intermarried with those of the Dukes of Devonshire. After the Battle of the Boyne, in 1690, King James II rested here before going into exile in France. It remains the property of the present Duke of Devonshire.

BALLYNAHINCH

Grace O'Malley, or Granuaile as she is known in Irish, was a fearless woman warrior who in the sixteenth century married Donal O'Flaherty, the builder of Ballynahinch Castle shown in this Currier and Ives print. It was the only fortification of Granuaile's kingdom built inland, since she was geared to the sea; her other castles were built along the coast.

When her husband died in 1570 while raiding Galway City, Granuaile, with the aid of her three sons, continued to expand her sea empire by developing a trade with Spain. Later, she married Burke of County Mayo. She was, of course, considered a pirate by the English and eventually they hunted her down, kidnapped her children, took possession of her ships, and left her with neither wealth nor influence. Her last years were spent in her castle on Clare Island at the entrance to Clew Bay, where she died of natural causes.

Opposite top:
BEAUTIES OF IRISH SCENERY—THE OLD WEIR BRIDGE, LAKES OF KILLARNEY

Opposite bottom:
THE VALLEY OF THE BLACKWATER

Next pages:
A SCENE IN OLD IRELAND

RAPIDS OF DOONASS—ON THE SHANNON

These rapids near the village of Castleconnell exist no more, that is, unless the engineer at Ardnacrusha opens the floodgates of a giant hydroelectric plant and for a brief interval the cataracts roar again at the Falls of Doonass as they did in the days of Currier and Ives.

In those bygone days salmon, some weighing forty or fifty pounds, danced in the pools as they fought their way upriver. If today the rapids are but a shadow of their former self and the fish are likewise reduced, the Shannon near Doonass is still one of the best angling spots in the world and still a place of wild beauty. The old-timers of the nearby village occasionally sing this song:

In Doonass I was born, and sure there I'd like to die,
And beneath St. Senan's Graveyard there my body for
  to lie,
And if fortune never forces me the stormy seas to cross
I'll dwell in Castleconnell near the Falls of Doonass.

From Castleconnell the best way to visit the scene in the print is to take O'Brien's Bridge and follow the road to Clonlara and then to Doonass. You will find the Anglers Rest Pub strategically situated on the river. Follow the footpath along its banks to the old castle ruins and enjoy the solitude.

THE CORK RIVER—NEAR GLANMIRE, COUNTY CORK

As the river winds around the coastal hills on its way to the ocean at the Cove of Cork it creates a picturesque setting for the village of Glanmire.

ISLAND OF
SAINTS AND HOLY PLACES

For centuries before Christianity came to Ireland, the second of February was a day of saturnalia, with sacred rites, torchlight parades, and noisy dances. A sense of revelry pervaded the atmosphere, and unrestrained merriment was widespread throughout the land. It was four hundred years before the pope felt secure enough in the Christian faith of the Irish people to suppress this ancient holy day and substitute the Feast of the Purification of the Blessed Virgin. Instead of marching in the torchlight processions, the people now filed quietly into their local churches to light candles on side altars. The people call it Candlemas Day. Long gone is the infectious feeling of joy and happiness with which the day had been originally celebrated.

The church was less successful with Samhain on November 1, when the sun died and the east wind blew. Then the powers of darkness could influence all things. Incantations would make the dead appear among the living to answer questions and tell of future events. The Christian church renamed this holiday All Saints Day. The older spirit of Halloween, however, lives on, especially in the heart of every child. It is a day when the young can dress as evil spirits and arrive on doorsteps to threaten those who don't provide them with goodies. The holiday may now be celebrated even more widely than in ancient times. These holidays and other religious practices clearly show that the Irish were deeply concerned about spiritual matters long before the arrival of Saint Patrick. His success may be due in part to the rites already practiced by the people under the leadership of their druidic priests.

The druids celebrated four great festivals that divided the year: February (Imbolc), May (Beltaine), midsummer (Lughnasa), and November (Samhain). They worshipped the sun, moon, and wind. They venerated trees, wells, rivers, and pillars of stone. Fire and water were the most sacred of all things. At the beginning of May, fires were lit in honor of the sun god. The first fire was lit at Howth, County Dublin, and then carried from village to village until all of Ireland was "on fire." (The custom of bonfires in Ireland is still common today.) Men jumped through the flames as a show of strength and the women jumped to win a speedy marriage. Finally the cattle were driven through the embers to insure their fertility. As the fires burned out and the celebration died down, everyone carried a piece of charred wood home to bring luck in the coming year. The sacred fire at Tara, the ancient capital of Ireland, was lit only every three years and wood from it was used to light holy fires throughout the country.

The Christian missionaries led by Saint Patrick were subtle. Rather than confrontation to discourage the old practices, other methods were used. Instead of uprooting them, sacred trees were left standing and sacrificial stones were left untouched. The old shrines were co-opted to the new religion: ancient holy places became sanctified by association with a saint's name and served as focuses of prayer. The ancient druidic practices were so strong that when Christianity won out, it was almost inevitable that the new religion would take on their strength and become identified with the Irish nation. In the early Middle Ages, when Christianity had taken hold, it was so powerful that it became a revolution that the Irish exported to the neighboring countries—Scotland, England, and beyond. Ireland was a beacon of light in those dark centuries, and the Irish missionary zeal is still very active in Africa, the Far East, and Central America.

The Irish have not entirely forgotten their origins. Some years ago, a forestry department official fired a group of workers who had refused to build a fence across an old druid mound. The entire population of Eire was incensed by this proposed sacrilege and the central government in Dublin quickly ordered the official to rehire the workers and build the fence away from the ancient shrine.

THE APOSTLE OF IRELAND
SAINT PATRICK

A great legend illustrates one aspect of Saint Patrick's method of preaching the new gospel:

Ossian, son of Finn MacCoumhall, fell in love with a beautiful fairy queen in the forest, who took him as her husband and brought him over the western sea to Tir Na N'Og (the land of the young). After he had been there what seemed a short time he became lonesome for his friends and comrades-in-arms back home in Ireland. The beautiful queen reluctantly let him ride back over the waves on a magnificent white steed with the warning that he had to stay on his horse or he could never return.

But Ireland had changed, and Ossian wandered aimlessly in the old haunts without finding his family or friends. On seeing a group of young men trying to move a large boulder he laughed at their weakness and, reaching down with one hand, he grabbed the boulder and threw it easily away. The effort broke the girth on his mount and he fell to the ground and was immediately transformed into a bewildered old man.

The year was 432 and the people, taking pity upon him, brought him to Saint Patrick who was preaching in the area. After hearing his story, Saint Patrick blessed Ossian and told him he could, indeed, go back to Tir Na N'Og, but instead of the beautiful princess to greet him, he would meet Christ his savior, and his family and friends together with the angels and saints. And so, as the rest of Ireland had been doing in his absence, Ossian was baptized and was thereby guaranteed to go to a beautiful place where he would live forever.

Clearly, Saint Patrick had a thorough knowledge of Ireland's myths, beliefs, and religious practices, and he adapted them to his mission—to bring Christianity to the Irish. Thus, for example, he appropriated the old Celtic new year (Halloween) as a Christian feast of All Saints Day or All Hallows. Likewise, under his guidance, many Celtic gods and goddesses were replaced by Christian saints who had similar attributes. Patrick's intimate knowledge of Irish lore and culture was gained long before he arrived to fulfill his ultimate mission. He had previously spent time in Ireland under very different circumstances.

Saint Patrick was born in Wales, perhaps in 372. His father, Calpurnius, was a member of the ruling class of Roman Britain, a rich landowner and a deacon of the Christian church. The Roman Empire at that time had conquered England and Wales but was unable to advance on the northern realm, Scotland. No attempt at all was made to conquer Ireland, which was called the Pagan Island and had the reputation of being a wild place populated by fierce warriors.

The reputation was well founded. On one occasion, a seafaring warrior called Niall of the Nine Hostages attacked the coast of Wales and carried off Patrick, who was then sixteen years old, making him a slave in County Down. Patrick herded sheep there for six years. He made friends, however, and got to know the people before finally making his escape and returning home. He vowed to come back. By his own account, he heard the Irish calling to him in a dream, crying out as if in one voice, "We entreat thee, holy youth, that thou come and henceafter walk among us."

Patrick did eventually return to conquer Ireland when Saint Germanus, Bishop of Auxerre, appointed him Bishop of the Irish, and financed an expedition to send him back with twenty-four companions to preach the gospel. The empire of the Romans is long gone, but Patrick's peaceful Christian conquest of Ireland survives to the present.

A number of legends grew around Saint Patrick's early success in preaching the gospel; they involve reports of miracles performed on behalf of early converts and curses visited upon those who opposed him. He was supposed to have turned a pack of vicious dogs to stone when they were set upon him by a man called Dichu. He changed himself and his followers into a herd of deer to escape capture by the druids (high priests of the old religion). His best-known miracle occurred after he had fasted for the forty days of Lent in County Mayo on a mountain now called Croagh Patrick. There, he "gathered together from all parts of Ireland, all the poisonous creatures. . . . By the power of the word he drove the whole pestilent swarm from the precipice of the mountain, headlong into the ocean—*Serpentes et omni venenata animalia ex Hibernia baculo Jesu expulit.*"

Less dramatic, but perhaps even more powerful were Patrick's gifts of persuasion. When challenged as to how there could be three persons, Father, Son, and Holy Ghost in one true God, he plucked a shamrock from the ground and held it up for all to see. There were three equal leaves on the one stem. From that day forward, the shamrock rivaled the ancient harp as the national symbol of Ireland.

The true power of Saint Patrick was as a dedicated and inspiring missionary. Knowing the Irish well from having lived among them, he was especially equipped to convert them. His strategy was to seek out their leaders. Once, on the eve of Beltaine, the celebration of the druid religion on May 1, he set a huge fire on a hill opposite the hill of Tara, Ireland's ancient capital near Dublin, to challenge the druid celebration on Tara. When he was brought before King Laoghaire, son of Niall of the Nine Hostages, for his impertinence he succeeded in converting the king along with many of the druids. He repeated this performance with a similar result before King Aengus of Munster at the Rock of Cashal in Tipperary. Thereafter, the success of Patrick's mission was virtually assured. As time went by, churches, abbeys, and monasteries, with their priests, bishops, and monks, grew like mushrooms in the morning mist.

Saint Patrick established the seat, the headquarters of his church in Ireland, on a hilltop in Armagh in the province of Ulster. There he would retire in his old age, after completing the conquest of the ancient druid religion of Ireland. Armagh today is in Northern Ireland, part of the United Kingdom, and occupied by British troops. It remains, however, united spiritually with Ireland as a whole: both the Catholic Cardinal of Ireland and the Protestant Primate of the Church of Ireland make their headquarters there.

THE HOLY WELL

In pre-Christian times the water from certain wells was considered to have healing power. These places became sacred fountains and also served as the locations for the performance of rites of worship. Among the legendary evidence of their druidic origins, however, are the verses reproduced below by John D. Frazer, a cabinetmaker and part-time poet who died in 1849.

Saint Patrick and his followers were unable to distract the peasantry from these sites, so they blessed them and began to use the water for the sacrament of baptism. As time went by the wells became more familiar as Christian symbols venerated by saints' names.

The ancient well shown in this Currier and Ives print became Saint Finian's Well.

The Holy Wells

The holy wells—the living wells—the cool, the fresh, the pure
A thousand ages rolled away, and still those founts endure,
As full and sparkling as they flowed, ere slave or tyrant trod,
The emerald garden, set apart for Irishmen by God!
And while their stainless chastity and lasting life have birth,
Amid the oozy cells and caves of gross, material earth,
The scripture of creation holds no fairer type than they
That an immortal spirt can be linked with human clay!
How sweet, of old, the bubbling gush—no less to antlered race,
Than to the hunter, and the hound, that smote them in the chase!
In forest depths the water-fount beguiled the Druids' love,
From that celestial fount of fire which warned from worlds above;
Inspired apostles took it for a center to the ring,
When sprinking round baptismal life—salvation—from the spring;
And in the sylvan solitude, or lonely mountain cave,
Beside it past the hermit's light, as stainless as its were.

THE SEVEN CHURCHES OF CLONMACNOISE

After Saint Patrick's work was completed a golden age of Christianity began in Ireland. It spread far beyond Ireland's shores, sending missionaries and scholars to establish learning institutions and monasteries throughout Scotland, northern England, and on the continent of Europe. Ireland became known as the Island of Saints and Scholars. At the core of this movement was Clonmacnoise, a Gaelic word meaning "The Secluded Recess of the Sons of Nobles."

Established in 534 by Saint Ciarnan, Clonmacnoise was a picturesque village built in the center of Ireland on the main water highway, the River Shannon, which winds its way to the sea from one hundred miles inland. The seven churches that were eventually built had connections to special benefactors, such as the Church of the O'Kellys, who were Kings of Connacht, and Finian's Church, named after Finian MacCarthy of the Royal Munster clan. Distinctive round towers were built at Clonmacnoise as places of refuge for the monks during raids on the settlement. Raiders could not knock down the towers because the walls of the base were too thick, nor could they get in because the entrance was twelve feet above the ground. Once inside the monks pulled their ladder up behind them. The round tower, as a defensive refuge, is found throughout Ireland.

Clonmacnoise developed an unusual mystique. Burial in Saint Ciarnan's city came to mean assurance of heavenly reward. Consequently, it is not surprising that Rory O'Connor, the last High King of Ireland, was buried within its walls in 1198. Virgal O'Rourke, a King of Connacht who built one of the round towers, also lies buried there. Religion, scholarship, and art flourished there. The Book of the Dun Cow, one of the most precious Irish medieval manuscripts, a rival to the Book of Kells, was produced there in the eleventh century. As a learning center, Clonmacnoise became known throughout the Christian world.

The great prestige of this religious settlement brought tremendous turmoil over the centuries. The riches it attracted caused much jealousy in the surrounding areas and also made it a tempting target for foreign invaders. In the year 720, and later in the same century, Clonmacnoise was burned in disputes with other Christian communities. The King of Cashal burned it in the year 830, and was slain there during a second attempt to burn it some time later. It is probable that in these years all the buildings were still made of wood. The Church of the Kings, which was built around 901, is believed to have been the first stone structure. By this time the Vikings had appeared on the scene. With their long, flat boats they found their way up the Shannon to loot the treasures of Clonmacnoise. From 830 to 1013 it was burned five times

THE ABBEY OF CLARE—GALWAY

by the Vikings, although sometimes with local help. At the Battle of Clontarf, however, in 1014, the Irish decisively defeated the Vikings and those invaders no longer took away the gold and silver chalices, drinking horns, and jewelry that was stored there.

Throughout its history Clonmacnoise was plundered more than fifty times. It was destroyed totally or partially at least twenty times. More than fifteen battles took place on the grounds of the churches and monastery. The English, a late-arriving menace, plundered the town in 1178 and many more times in subsequent years, taking vestments, books, chalices, linen, and other cloths. In 1552 Clonmacnoise was finally destroyed as a living settlement forever. The destruction is described in the *Annals of the Four Masters:* "Clonmacnoise was plundered and devastated by the English of Athlone; they took the large bells out of the cloigtheach [the steeple or belfry] and left neither large nor small bell image, altar, book, gem, nor even glass in a window in the walls of a church that they did not carry away with them; and that

truly it was a lamentable deed, to plunder the City of Kiernan, the Patron Saint."

As a living settlement Clonmacnoise lasted one thousand years, but in many ways it is still alive and remains the heart and soul of Ireland. Pope John Paul II visited there in 1979. Busloads of tourists crowd into the village during the summer, seeking a touch of the spirit and magic of the past.

The scene depicted in the print looks entirely the same today, except for a visitor's center and bookstore. A few cows graze the fields on the banks of the Shannon against the backdrop of the village ruins. You can sit in the same spot as the people in the print and detect no change in the hundred or so years since the print was made. The castle in the left foreground was built in the year 1200 to protect the monastery and the approaches to the Shannon. The cause of its destruction is unknown but it has remained as depicted for some 250 years. Walking around this historic area one has the feeling that the spirit of Clonmacnoise will survive forever.

The Abbey of the Holy Cross— Tipperary

In the year 1110 Pope Pascal II presented a piece of the true cross to Murtagh O'Brien, who was then the High King of Ireland. The wood was set in gold and adorned with precious stones. Cistercian monks preserved the relic in the Abbey of the Holy Cross on the River Suit near the small village of Holy Cross in County Tipperary. Huge crowds flocked to the shrine during the Middle Ages to view the relic. It was, however, removed for safety by the monks during the Reformation and was apparently lost at that time.

Today the Abbey of the Holy Cross has been restored as a national monument and is again visited by thousands of pilgrims each year. On a side altar, enclosed in a small display case with a circular glass center, is a piece of wood one-inch long and a half-inch wide. The sign says that the wood is a remnant of the true cross on which Jesus of Nazareth was crucified.

Right:
Our Lady of Knock—County Mayo

Below:
The Abbey of the Holy Cross—Tipperary

BRIAN BORÚ
MONARCH OF IRELAND AND HERO OF CLONTARF

After Saint Patrick's religion had been firmly established for more than 350 years, it had to withstand an assault from a different kind of paganism. This took the form of an external threat posed by the arrival of the Vikings. These warriors, both the Danes and Norsemen known as the Men of the Bays, began to arrive in Ireland in small bands at the end of the eighth century. Reaching the coast, they moved quickly with sail and paddle up the shallow rivers. Clad in coats of mail and swinging battle-axes, they left terror in their wake.

The Vikings had already overrun England, great parts of France, and Northern Europe. They had penetrated through the Bosporus up to the Volga and even threatened Greece and Turkey. Their advance on Ireland was slow, however, despite the fact that it was only a few days sail away. One of the reasons was that the Vikings tended to settle down and to marry with the Irish.

In 832 there was a strong Norwegian push as the famous warrior Tuirgeis, with a force of 120 ships and ten thousand warriors, sailed up the rivers Boyne and Liffey. He cut Ireland in two, going as far as Athlone in the west and taking over Armagh, Saint Patrick's capital, in the north.

Tuirgeis was recognized as king by the foreign elements scattered throughout the country, but he was unable to consolidate his gains. Many Gaelic chieftains remained independent. In 845 one of them, Malachy of Meath, succeeded in kidnapping Tuirgeis and executing him. Norwegian influence was further destroyed at a great battle with Danes in 1850 at Carlingford Loch.

In the tenth century, the Danes consolidated their gains along the eastern coast by taking possession of large parts of the interior, but they provoked fierce resistance by their sacking of Clonmacnoise in 914. As time went by the strongest resistance to the Danes was centered in the Christian kingdoms of Meath in the center of the country adjacent to Dublin and Thomond in the south, comprising the present-day counties of Clare, Limerick, and Tipperary with its ecclesiastical center at Cashel.

In 941 a child was born who would become one of Ireland's greatest heroes. He was Brian, son of Kennedy, chief of Thomond, and he came to life in the small town of Borime, near Killaloe on the bank of the River Shannon. He later became known as Brian Ború. Brian's oldest brother, Mahon, became king of all Munster in 968 and was continually at war with the Danes and the Gaelic rulers of Leinster. In 976 Mahon was slain by the Danes and Brian succeeded him. Malachy II, a Gaelic chieftain of the kingdom of Meath defeated a force of Danes at Tara in 980 and proclaimed himself Emperor of Ireland. In time they split the country between them; Malachy ruled the northern half and Brian the south.

Brian was a warrior chieftain, a good general. Strong and fierce in battle, he had an iron will and a great ambition to rule all of Ireland. His royal seat was at Kincora, near the Shannon, and he extended his reign across most of the country subduing Gaelic and Danish kingdoms alike. He championed Christianity and won the alliance of the Viking population who had embraced the faith. By 1005, his support was so overwhelming that Malachy was persuaded to withdraw as co-emperor of Ireland. Brian did not, however, totally succeed in overcoming Sihtric, the Viking king of Dublin, and the Gaelic rulers of Leinster, one of Ireland's four provinces.

In 1014 an army of Vikings assembled to oppose Brian Ború at Clontarf near the Liffey, in what is today the city center of Dublin. The force consisted of twenty thousand warriors from all parts of the Viking domain together with native Vikings from Ireland and Gaelic chieftains aligned with Sihtric. Relying primarily on men from Munster and Connacht, and local Christian Vikings, Brian Ború met the Vikings with an almost equal number, armed with sword and crucifix. Now seventy-three years old, he was persuaded to retire to his tent, leaving the generalship of the battle to his son Murchadh.

The Vikings had the better of it in the early fighting, but the Irish held on throughout the day. Both sides moved back and forth. Toward evening Malachy of Meath arrived. Despite having been deposed by Brian Ború, Malachy was unselfish in his patriotism for Ireland and the strong support that he deployed proved decisive. With their backs to the sea and the River Liffey the Vikings found that the rising tide had moved their long ships offshore: seven thousand were slain.

The victory was costly to the Irish, however, as Brian Ború was slain in his tent by a fleeing Viking; his son Murchadh and a grandson also lost their lives. But the battle ended the Viking threat to Ireland and broke their power on the continent of Europe as well. Many of the defeated warriors settled down, converting to Christianity as others of their race had already done. In due course, with their red and blond hair and fair features, they became more Irish than the Irish themselves. Thereafter Malachy II became the high king and his successors experienced a period of approximately 160 years of independence and the freedom to fight among themselves until the invasion of Henry II of England in 1171.

THE BATTLES
FOR INDEPENDENCE
AND RELIGIOUS FREEDOM

On September 23, 1601, Don Juan Del Aquila and twenty-five hundred Spanish soldiers landed at Kinsale on the southern coast of Ireland. Del Aquila was immediately besieged by an English army led by Lords Mountjoy and Carew. Why Spanish and English soldiers should have been doing battle in Ireland may seem strange, but sections of Ireland had been occupied at that time for about four hundred years by various neighbors from across the sea. After ruling England for a hundred years, the Normans, led by the Earl of Pembroke, commonly known as Strongbow, invaded Ireland in 1170. They were followed by increasing waves of English invaders. In 1541, English monarchs began calling themselves Kings of Ireland. Thus, the Spaniard Del Aquila landed in the middle of an English stronghold.

These were the final days of the reign of Elizabeth I, Queen of England by succession and Queen of Ireland by the sword. Her father, Henry VIII, had incurred the wrath of Catholic Spain when he divorced his first wife, Catherine of Aragon, who had failed to bear a son, to marry Anne Boleyn. Elizabeth, the child of that union, was her father's daughter and vowed to keep her empire Protestant and free from the designs of Spain. In England itself, a country that would change its religion by royal decree five times in thirty years, the first was a relatively simple task, but Ireland adhered strongly to Catholicism and its Gaelic leaders united as one to resist conversion from the older faith and to contest English claims to sovereignty.

Led by Hugh O'Neill and Hugh O'Donnell from Ulster in the north, the Irish rebelled. In what became known as the Nine Years War, they defeated every English force thrown against them in battle, including twenty thousand men under the queen's favorite, the Earl of Essex. Now, in 1601, came the reason for Del Aquila's presence in Ireland. The rebels hoped to push Elizabeth and the English out of Ireland forever with Spanish help. O'Neill and O'Donnell hurriedly marched south to surround the last British force on the island, the army of Mountjoy and Carew that was besieging the Spanish general at Kinsale.

O'Neill was a brave soldier, a shrewd diplomat, and a brillant general, with a deep capacity for caution. He was confident that he could outwit Elizabeth's forces and was content to hold his position, cutting off Mountjoy and Carew from supplies from the country while Del Aquila kept them from getting supplies by sea. But Spanish blood was impatient and pressure from the Spanish general persuaded O'Neil to attack prematurely. Furthermore, Mountjoy and Carew were not without guile. They sent informers posing as deserters filtering into Kinsale, filling the town with stories of the supposed desperation and plight of the British troops besieging the city. It was a ruse, and when O'Neill attacked he saw English formations ready and waiting for him. He knew that he had been misled and made a hasty decision to hold back but his orders only resulted in confusion. This permitted the English cavalry to break through his lines and the battle was lost.

The rebellion was defeated and Catholic Ireland was at the mercy of the Protestant monarch. O'Neill retreated to Ulster and a few years later was forced into exile. Del Aquila surrendered and was sent back to Spain where he was court-martialed for incompetency. Elizabeth died soon thereafter, but her successor, James I, used the failed rebellion to punish O'Neill and O'Donnell and their followers—the backbone of the resistance of Gaelic Ireland. They lost their lands in Ulster by a royal decree and large numbers of Scottish and English settlers were brought in to take their places. Unlike their earlier Norman and English counterparts, the vast majority of descendants of these predominently Scottish Presbyterian settlers, who in time grew to become one-fifth of Ireland's population, never gave their loyalty to the country in which they lived. So it was that England was able to keep the upper hand in the various battles that followed.

The Currier and Ives prints in this section pick up the history from this time forward, as Ireland alternated in seeking its freedom by force of arms and peaceful means. At the Battle of the Boyne in 1690, the descendants of these Ulster settlers became, in effect, a gigantic fifth column. They aided William III (another foreigner, from the Dutch House of Orange) in his successful battles to conquer all of Ireland for England and the Protestant faith. The fight for religious freedom in the south could be said to have been won later in Daniel O'Connell's time, and the fight for political freedom would continue up to the present day. The Anglo-Irish Protestant upper classes also aligned themselves for the most part with British rule, though from time to time some of their members, men such as Robert Emmet and Theobald Wolf Tone, led rebellions for Irish freedom; others such as Charles Stewart Parnell campaigned for peaceful change.

THE BATTLE OF THE BOYNE

On July 1, 1690, a battle was fought on a stream called the Boyne about fifteen miles north of Dublin. It flows through the village of Oldbridge, to Drogheda, and then on to the Irish Sea. It was there that an English king called James II, who was Catholic, attempted to regain the English throne after being deposed by a parliament that wished to keep England Protestant. William of Orange, monarch of the Netherlands, had been invited to succeed him.

For the engagement at the Boyne, James mustered an army of twenty-five thousand men, composed primarily of Irish and French volunteers. Many of the Irish hoped to regain land that had previously been confiscated by the English. William, meanwhile, had landed in Belfast from Holland and marched south with an army of British colonials (local Irish Protestants of English and Scottish ancestry), French Huguenots, and Dutch Protestants. The Dutch numbered eight thousand men in an army of thirty-five thousand strong.

King James cut a dashing figure and had a reputation as a brave soldier; William, considered an ugly man, had the advantage of numbers and a better-equipped army, with a clear-cut superiority in artillery. Further counting

against him, James had failed to inspire the Irish: it had become clear before the battle that he intended to remain king of Ireland as well as England. It was apparent to the Irish that a victory at the Boyne would not lead to a free Ireland, only to a Catholic one. In the event, Ireland would gain neither political or religious freedom at this battle.

On the day of the battle William brought his army to the north side of the river. James was on the south side at the village of Oldbridge. William first deceived James by making a feint at Rosnaree, which was five miles inland, when he moved eight thousand men in that direction. James moved the bulk of his army to oppose this threat, leaving four thousand men at Oldbridge. They were attacked by fifteen thousand of William's troops, spearheaded by the elite Blue Guards of Holland.

The Irish attacked them in the river, but the Dutch, armed to the teeth with muskets, bayonets, and primitive hand grenades, spread devastation before them and secured the south bank, dislodging the Irish from the village of Oldbridge. Great numbers of the Irish, armed only with scythes and pointed sticks, fell back in disarray toward Dublin. Along the way they met King James and the main part of his army, which had never fired a shot. James failed to rally his troops and fled to Dublin. When James reached Dublin, he met Lady TirConnell, the wife of his army chief, and complained bitterly to her about the failure of the Irish to fight: "Your countrymen, madam, can run well." "Not so well as your majesty, for I see you have won the race," she is said to have replied.

A few days later he left for France and the protection of his ally, Louis XIV, never to return again. The Irish did run well that day, suffering only one thousand casualties to five hundred on the English side.

The actual battle as fought at the Boyne was strictly between the Irish and the Dutch. The French units saw no action on behalf of King James, and the Protestant Irish and English engaged in little or no action for King William. In a way the flight of James made it simple for the Irish, who retreated and regrouped under the Duke of Berwick and Patrick Sarsfield at Limerick.

Currier and Ives made two similar prints of the Battle of the Boyne. There are differences in the compositions, although one is obviously copied from the other, and both depict the actual crossing of King William after his troops had secured the south bank. Just prior to William's crossing, fire from his cannons killed the Irish lord Walter Dongan, whose regiment of dragoons opposed the Dutch. A group of Irish dragoons braved a withering fire to retrieve the body of their leader. (I believe this is the scene depicted in the lower right of the print.)

The confusion of colored uniforms in the prints is historically accurate. The Dutch regiments wore both yellow and red, and many other regiments on both sides wore red uniforms. This made things dangerous even for victorious soldiers, some of whom were injured by their own side. Each group, however, wore distinctive badges of identification at the Boyne. Ironically, the Inniskillen Protestant regiment, which is the pride of modern Orangemen, wore a sprig of green in their hats that day.

Irish Protestants, the vast majority being of the Presbyterian faith, today celebrate this battle as their greatest victory over the Catholic Irish. Each year they march in the thousands all over Northern Ireland in commemoration of this great victory; pictures of King Billy adorn every Protestant household. Lost somewhere in the shuffle of history is the aftermath of King William's victory, for he completely suppressed the Presbyterian faith, not to mention the Catholic one, in Ireland in favor of the Anglican church, the official church of England. Presbyterians became known as "dissenters." This turn of events forced upward of 250,000 Irish Presbyterians (the so-called Scotch-Irish) to emmigrate to America after the Battle of the Boyne. Some of them went on to become the backbone of George Washington's army in the fight for freedom from England in the United States. Eighteen descendants of those immigrants would eventually become presidents of the United States, including Andrew Jackson, who was born on the way across the Atlantic, and who, ironically, would defeat the English at the Battle of New Orleans in 1812.

KING WILLIAM III

THE BOYNE WATER

The River Boyne is far from Belfast, where the significance of the battle is still the most emotional issue for Irish men and women of the Protestant faith.

That King William and his army did not have much difficulty in fording the river is demonstrated by the cattle in the print not even being up to their knees in water. The level of the Boyne on July 1, 1690, made it easy to cross. William's troops probably were up to their waists and no more, holding their muskets above their heads. Had James kept the bulk of his army intact at Oldbridge, the crossing of the Boyne could have been disastrous for the Dutch. James certainly had the advantage of defending a fixed position, even though his troops lacked adequate weapons.

On July 12, 1990, almost exactly three hundred years after the event, thousands of Protestants from Northern Ireland had hoped to congregate at the Boyne. The intention was to celebrate, as the nineteenth-century patriot John Mitchel wrote in his journal in jail, "the Victory of the Dutch King of England over their own countrymen." However, the strong possibility of a "donnybrook" led to the cancellation of the plans.

LONDONDERRY: ON THE RIVER FOYLE

With their tanks and guns, Oh my God, what have they done
To the town I love so well
Contemporary song by Phil Coulter

With its quiet pastoral scene this Currier and Ives print belies the conflict this town has witnessed. Before it was Londonderry there was a monastic site here named Derry, and there begins another tale of two cities.

Derry was part of the lands of an Ulster Gaelic chieftain named Red Hugh O'Donnell. As already noted, he and a countryman, Hugh O'Neill, were defeated in 1601 by Elizabethan forces. They were forced to leave Ireland in 1607, in what became known as "The Flight of the Earls." England then decided to push out the natives and settle the area with people from the lowlands of Scotland who were mostly of the Presbyterian faith. For their protection, on the west side of the River Foyle a magnificent walled plantation city was built by the Irish Society of London under a charter from King James I. It was called London's Derry. The walls enclosing the city were six feet thick and twenty feet tall and remain intact to this day in the city center.

In 1688, before the Battle of the Boyne, the Catholic Irish forces of King James II approached Londonderry. The leader, Lord Mountjoy, ordered the Protestant troops to withdraw from within and allow the Catholic army to enter the city. Colonel Robert Lundy agreed to surrender his forces to the troops of King James, but before the Catholics could enter the city thirteen young Protestant apprentice boys from the local trades rushed up and slammed the gates shut in the face of the approaching army. This courageous act turned the sentiment of the city against King James and a three-and-a-half-month siege followed. The siege was finally lifted when a fleet loyal to King William broke through a boom on the River Foyle. The Catholic army, almost as starved as the Protestant defenders, was forced to retire.

When King William returned to England to begin his rule, after defeating the Catholic forces at the Battle of the Boyne and elsewhere, Ulster Presbyterians who had fought with him were surprised to find their faith now discriminated against in favor of the Anglican church. Many of the defenders of Londonderry, together with other Ulster Protestants, decided to leave for the United States and Londonderry became their port of exit. Tens of thousands of them made their way to Boston, Charleston, and Philadelphia. The towns of Derry and Londonderry in New Hampshire were founded by these immigrants before the American Revolution.

A small Catholic population had remained behind when King James's forces departed from Londonderry. As time went by, they were joined in dribs and drabs by others who had fled to the mountains in nearby County Donegal. They eked out a living by doing the menial work that Protestants would not do, and built shacks in the marshy area around the city. The Catholics encountered few problems as long as they did not oppose British rule.

This marshy settlement, by then known as Bogside, burst onto the pages of the world's newspapers in 1969, when its inhabitants, demanding equal rights, fought a heavily armed body of Protestant paramilitary police. On January 30, 1972, at a street corner in the Bogside, thirteen young Catholic men marching for civil rights were shot dead. Some of them were apprentice boys in the local trades. The irony of history had come full circle.

In the centuries following the first siege of the walled city, its Catholic inhabitants had come to outnumber the Protestants by more than two to one. Despite this, Protestants had continued to rule the city. Finally, in the 1970s, the British were forced to adopt electoral reforms that gave the descendants of King James's army control of the city government. In 1984 they renamed the administration the Derry City Council, but continued to call the city Londonderry in deference to the feelings of the Protestant minority.

THE SIEGE OF LIMERICK

They have sent for fresh artillery,
The guns are on the way.
"God help our hapless Limerick
When dawns another day."
Thus speaks the gallant Sarsfield,
As sadly he recalls
The famine and despair that lurk
Behind those crumbling walls.

And yet one blow for freedom—
One daring midnight ride:
And William may be humbled yet,
For all his power and pride!
"Go! Bring to me 'The Galloper,'"
To Highway Hogan say,
'Tis Ireland hath need of him,
And him alone to-day!

From the poem "Galloping O'Hogan"
by Percy French

The quick flight of James II after the Battle of the Boyne convinced the Irish that he had no feeling for their cause but simply wanted to use them for his own personal gain.

Since he had found no English army to fight for him, his only choice had been an Irish one. But the Irish quickly forgot James and decided to fight their own battle against King William at Limerick. Patrick Sarsfield, who had not particularly distinguished himself at the Boyne, emerged as the inspiring military leader in the struggle.

Limerick, which began as a Viking settlement in the tenth century, was the second largest city in Ireland at the time. It straddles the River Shannon between County Clare and County Limerick. The Shannon divides into two parts north of the city and unites again south of the city, thus creating a large island where King John had built a castle in 1210 near Thomond Bridge. Huge, strong stone walls, remnants of which survive to this day, gave Limerick some tough defenses. The defenders, numbering some fourteen thousand soldiers, were poorly armed, although they had some cannons and muskets. The army included a cavalry and dragoon regiment.

As the print tells us William arrived before Limerick on August 8, 1690 and by the end of August, his army was still trying to storm the walls. The defense of Limerick involved all residents of the city. Men, women, children, and priests did their part alongside the soldiers.

THE RIVER SHANNON FROM THE TOWER OF LIMERICK CATHEDRAL

Sarsfield, with his scout, The Galloping O'Hogan, led a daring raid behind the English lines; four hundred calvary and two hundred dragoons attacked William's artillery and siege train at Ballyneety. They wiped out the English and blew up the munitions, except for small amounts they were able to carry back to Limerick.

The key to military victory for Sarsfield was good intelligence. He actually gained entry to the English camp after learning that the password for King William's troops was none other than his own name. The poem by Percy French tells the tale and the road signs today proudly mark the way between the Silvermine and Keeper mountains where Sarsfield rode.

On August 29 William gave up the siege and returned to England after losing five thousand soldiers. Irish losses were about one thousand. Victory for the Irish was in sight the following year, but their luck ran out at a place called Aughrim in Galway. There, under the leadership of the French general St. Ruth, the Irish lost their most decisive battle ever, with seven thousand soldiers slain. The remnants of the army fell back again on Limerick and a second siege was taken up, lasting from August 25 until September 23. It ended with Sarsfield signing the Treaty of Limerick. He was permitted to take twelve thousand of his officers and men and went into exile to join five thousand already in France, Spain, and Austria. This exodus was called the Flight of the Wild Geese. It began a tradition of taking Ireland's best to fight in foreign wars, but many children of the Wild Geese would become famous in the adopted lands of their fathers. One such individual was Marshall MacMahon, president of the French republic from 1873 to 1879 and the subject of a Currier and Ives print. Sarsfield himself would die in Holland in the French army fighting King William at the Battle of Neerwinden, where he would lament that he wished his blood had been shed for Ireland. In Ireland itself, the people would not rise again until 1798, when the United Irishmen and Theobald Wolf Tone led a combined Protestant and Catholic army against English rule. It was the first and only time such an event ever happened in Ireland.

Patrick Sarsfield, considered the greatest Irish military leader of all time, can reasonably be identified in the print on page 38 as the officer with sword and plumed hat at the left side. The ancient flag of Ireland (green with the gold harp) is to his left. It is dramatic in its domination of the print.

GLENGARIFF INN

The famous English writer William Makepeace Thackeray, while collecting literary and artistic material, visited Glengariff Inn in 1842. He was moved to write about it: "Within five miles round the pretty inn of Glengariff there is a country, of the magnificence of which no pen can give an idea."

Beautiful it may be, but the Gaelic Gleann Garbh means bitter glen and bitter it was for a French naval fleet of forty-five ships in 1796. The fleet's mission was to put 14,750 troops ashore in the inner sanctum of Bantry Bay near Glengariff. They had been sent by France to help Ireland free itself from the yoke of England, just as France had earlier helped America gain its freedom at Yorktown.

Glengariff and nearby Garish Island, with its lush palm trees warmed by the Gulf Stream, are considered the Florida of Ireland. The area gets the country's balmiest weather, even in winter. But that year the invading armada ran into gale-force winds at the mouth of the bay that scattered its vessels far and wide. Of the forty-five ships that sailed, only fourteen made it into Bantry Bay. They waited there without disembarking any soldiers for the other ships to arrive. After a few days of waiting they gave up and returned to France. Ironically, there was virtually no force to oppose them on the shore, because the British believed the cover story that the armada was bound for Portugal.

On board the *Indomptable,* with its eighty guns, was Theobald Wolf Tone, a Protestant adventurer from Dublin who was a friend to the Catholic masses. Tone had single-handedly convinced revolutionary France to send the fleet. About the unexpected outcome to the invasion he would note in his diary: "Well, England has had not such an escape since the Spanish Armada, and that expedition, like ours, was defeated by the weather; the elements fight against us, and courage is here to no avail."

Opposite:
ROBERT EMMET

ROBERT EMMET

Robert Emmet was a dangerous man. For his time, he was probably the most dangerous man alive. An Irish Protestant, he led a body of Irish Catholic city dwellers of Dublin in a rebellion against the greatest empire of its day.

All should have been quiet in 1803 when Emmet came on the scene. The great Irish rebellions of 1798, inspired by the French Revolution, had been completely suppressed and the Act of Union of 1801 had eliminated the Irish parliament in Dublin, combining it with the parliament in London.

Emmet and his army attacked Dublin Castle (seat of the empire in Ireland). The attorney general was killed. Terrorism of the worst and bloody kind. The rebellion was, of course, a failure and a few days later Emmet was captured and tried for treason.

The trial was a trauma both for the court and the establishment, because the authorities were confronted with the task of punishing one of their own brightest and most eloquent children. After all, Robert Emmet, the son of a leading physician, was just twenty-five years old and a student at Trinity College, at that time a bastion of Protestant education and English supremacy in Ireland.

Emmet called out from the dock: "I wish to procure for my country, the guarantee which Washington procured for America." A most dangerous man, indeed. His last words from the dock still haunt the governments of Ireland and England: "Let no man write my epitaph, for as no man who knows my motives dare now vindicate them, let them and me rest in obscurity and peace, and my name remain uninscribed until other times and other men can do justice to my character. When my country takes her place among the nations of the earth, then and not til then, let my epitaph be written." Interruption of these words by the presiding judge, Lord Norbury, caused him to comment: "My Lords you seem impatient for the sacrifice."

Emmet was quickly hanged and beheaded. As if that was not enough, he was drawn and quartered before a huge crowd on the streets of Dublin. He did not die in vain, however, becoming in many ways more dangerous after his death. His speech from the dock lived on in the hearts of his countrymen and on the lips of its most ardent nationalists at home and abroad. Some time later, in a log cabin in Kentucky, by the dim light of a fire, a young boy read Emmet's speech from the dock. Some day he, too, would make an inspiring speech. He did at a place called Gettysburg. His name was Abraham Lincoln.

EMMET'S BETROTHED

After the rebellion, Emmet escaped to the Wicklow Mountains. His friends advised him to leave the country immediately, but he would hear none of it. He had to return for one last time to Dublin to see Sarah Curran, youngest daughter of a celebrated barrister, John Philpot Curran. He failed to see his fiancée, however, and was subsequently arrested on August 25, 1803.

Opposite top:
LUGGELAW—COUNTY WICKLOW

Opposite bottom:
THE DARGLE GLEN—COUNTY WICKLOW

That there are roads for tourists today into the Valley of the Luggelaw and the Dargle Glen is due to the exploits of the "outlaw" Michael Dwyer and his gallant comrades. County Wicklow's proximity to Dublin and the Pale, combined with its inaccessibility, made this wild domain the perfect country for guerrilla warfare. Michael Dwyer and his band were poised to strike with Robert Emmet in 1803, but the general rebellion was called off because the organizers failed to ignite the people of Dublin.

Dwyer and his men were hunted high and low in the Valley of the Luggelaw and the Dargle Glen, but always kept one step ahead of the military. One fateful night, however, Dwyer and three comrades were surrounded by a hundred troops while resting in a small cottage in the Glen of Imaal. One of the men, who had been wounded, stood in the door to draw the soldier's fire while Dwyer and his two remaining friends dashed forth. Only Dwyer made it:

> Up sprang the three survivors for whom the hero
>   died,
> But only Michael Dwyer broke through the ranks
>   outside.
> He baffled his pursuers, who followed like the
>   wind:
> He swam the River Slaney and left them far
>   behind;
> But many an English soldier he promised soon
>   should fall,
> For those, his gallant comrades, who died in wild
>   Imaal.

And so they built their roads and fortifications in the glens of Wicklow, including the barracks at Glencree in the Dargle Glen, and eventually Michael surrendered and was banished for the rest of his life to Australia.

Should you travel in County Wicklow today, you can seek Saint Kevin's stone chapel at Glendalough opposite the Valley of the Luggelaw. You can follow the River Dargle to where it rises high in the valley between War Hill and Tonduff. There you will see the river tumble over the three-hundred-foot Powerscourt Waterfall to a winding narrow gorge lined with oak until it reaches the Irish Sea at Bray. Then you will understand why men like Michael Dwyer would fight so hard for this beautiful country.

DANIEL O'CONNELL: THE CHAMPION OF FREEDOM

Daniel O'Connell found Sir Robert Peel, Chief Secretary of Ireland and a famous Tory politician of the era, "this tough, squeezed out of the workings of I know not what factory in England . . . sent here before he got over the foppery of perfumed hankerchiefs and thin shoes . . . a lad ready to vindicate anything or everything." O'Connell had a way with words and in the rough and tumble politics of the day he could neutralize an opponent with a caustic comment on his character. When he perceived Peel as favoring the Northern Irish Protestant community, he dubbed him Orange Peel. But on January 22, 1815, O'Connell went too far when he referred to the Dublin Corporation (the local administration of the city) as that "beggarly corporation of Dublin."

He was immediately challenged to a duel by John D'Esterre, a member who wished to avenge the insult. It was a setup. Perceived by the establishment as getting too big for his britches, O'Connell had to be stopped. John D'Esterre, a Limerick Protestant officer in the Royal Marines, with a record of great bravery under enemy fire and known to be "one of the surest shots that ever fired a pistol," was the chosen assassin. It was a time when gentlemen lived or died by the duel. Many a promising career was cut short or advanced, as in the case of Lord Norbury, by skill with a dueling pistol. O'Connell, whose reputation was suffering because of his avoidance of duels, felt forced to accept this one. Hundreds of spectators watched in the snow as D'Esterre's shot for once missed its target and O'Connell's bullet ended a life.

Daniel O'Connell was born on the eve of the American Revolution in 1775 in Cahirciveen, County Kerry, Ireland, to parents who were modest landowners. He had a bachelor uncle, Maurice, nicknamed Hunting Cap, who owned a large estate called Derrynane Abbey (the subject of a Currier and Ives print). Uncle Cap adopted Daniel as his own son, and eventually left him all his wealth when he died at the age of ninety-six. Another uncle, who led an Irish regiment in the French Army, became a count of France. All were Catholics. Uncle Cap paid for Daniel to receive a Catholic school education in France, though the boy had to leave there in a hurry in 1793 when the French Revolution inconveniently closed the schools. Thereafter, O'Connell was educated in England, where he was admitted to the London bar and took his place as an excellent barrister and an up-and-coming orator.

In O'Connell's youth Ireland was a country with a large Catholic population ruled by a small Protestant aristocracy. Though it had its own parliament for local

affairs, it was largely subservient to the British parliament and to the king. The various geographic areas of Ireland were represented in this limited law-making body through boroughs. The representative of each borough to the parliament was invariably the owner of the most land in the region. In some areas there were freeholders, or other persons who were eligible to vote if they were rich enough. However, of the thirty-three districts into which the country was divided, eighteen were "pocket" or "rotten" boroughs, with no freeholders at all. (This system survived in a limited form up to the 1970s in Northern Ireland, where by virtue of their wealth individuals had up to six votes in the local parliament. Reforms finally made election to this parliament based on one man, one vote.)

Ireland's parliament voted itself out of existence in 1801 and most of its members were returned to the British parliament in London under the so-called Act of Union between the two countries. Catholics, however, had been effectively excluded from both parliaments, because in order to be a member they would have to take an oath denouncing the Mass, the Virgin Mary, the saints and other church beliefs. Daniel O'Connell's historical achievement in gaining Catholic emancipation for Ireland was that he succeeded in causing the British to lift the requirement of this oath in 1829. He was probably helped in this reform by the fact that it happened during the brief term of the Duke of Wellington as prime minister of Britain. Wellington himself had been born in Dublin, and when he defeated Napoleon at Waterloo, he had a number of Catholic regiments fighting by his side. It is doubtful that O'Connell would have gained anything under Robert "Orange" Peel, who later became prime minister.

That some Catholics could now manage to be elected to the British parliament meant little in the lives of millions of peasants, whose life-style was not changed by this emancipation. But the Catholic masses were impressed that O'Connell, a Catholic like themselves, managed to get himself elected in County Clare and that he had forced the British to change their rules. On top of this they admired the fact that he had the gift of gab, could hold his own in any public forum, and could wheel and deal with the best that the English had to offer. This led them to see O'Connell as their champion. He even came to believe it himself, and would sign his name "Daniel O'Connell, Liberator of Ireland." Even so, Ireland in his lifetime remained an oppressed nation.

Catholic emancipation was very important to one institution in Ireland, the Catholic church. Before 1800 the church had forged its own alliance with Britain in order to achieve some freedom of worship, and in return the church's activities were not persecuted. In fact, the British had established a seminary for Catholic priests in Maynooth, County Kildare, with the object of producing local priests who would not be tainted by foreign ideas of revolution. In 1823, the church forged an alliance with O'Connell, and the parish priests formed an organization called the Catholic Association, which collected funds for O'Connell's election campaigns and later for other Catholic candidates.

In the second half of his career, O'Connell devoted his energies to repealing the Act of Union, and he marshaled most of the population of the country in peaceful protests. His aim was to reestablish a local Irish parliament, while still remaining within the United Kingdom. But his efforts ended in failure. Successive meetings throughout the country attended by hundreds of thousands of people at each event were to reach a crescendo at a planned public rally on October 8, 1843, at Clontarf, Dublin. (It was there, in 1014, that Brian Ború had defeated the Vikings.) But on October 7, the day before the meeting was to take place, Prime Minister Peel declared it illegal and O'Connell backed away and cancelled it. To many of his followers, who had visions of pushing the British out of Ireland, O'Connell's capitulation proved the death knell for his nonviolent movement.

A number of young men in O'Connell's group had been making their mark while waiting for him to fall. Men such as Thomas Davis, William Smith O'Brien, Gavan Duffy, John Mitchel, and Thomas Francis Meagher. They published a newspaper, the *Nation*, which justified revolution under certain conditions. This group called themselves Young Ireland and included both Catholics and Protestants, but their hero was Theobald Wolf Tone (about whom, more later), whose motto had been to eliminate the words Catholic, Protestant, or Dissenter and substitute the common name of Irishman in their place. They challenged O'Connell's achievements and a poem appeared in their newspaper implying that O'Connell was a coward:

Who fears to speak of ninety-eight?
Who blushes at the name?
When cowards mock the patriots' fate
Who hangs his head with shame?
He's all a knave or half of a slave
Who slights his country thus,
But a true man, like you, man,
Will fill your glass with us.

At the age of seventy-two O'Connell's health failed: whether from the failure of the Clontarf meeting or from a brain tumor was unclear. But as 1845 drew to a close, famine struck the land, and he could clearly see the calamity that lay ahead. A shell of the man he had been, hunched over and in a whispered voice, he made his last address to the "Mother of Parliaments." Pleading for action to save his countrymen from starvation before one million of his people died, he found himself greeted only by stony silence from his fellow MPs. He knew that death

THE O'CONNELL FUNERAL PARADE IN NEW YORK

was close and he packed his bags and set out on a pilgrimage to Rome, a Catholic to the end. He made it only to Genoa, where he died on May 15, 1847. There, his heart was removed and sent to Rome; his body was returned to Ireland.

O'Connell has remained larger than life at home and abroad. While his methods failed and it was violence that ultimately freed his native land, historians agree that it was O'Connell's vision of Ireland that came forth, insofar as it is a Catholic one cut off from its main Protestant population. Some historians claim that the vast immigrant population of the United States had little sympathy for O'Connell's brand of politics. They are probably mistaken. Currier and Ives issued at least ten different prints showing him as the *Champion of Freedom,* the *Liberator,* and the *Champion of Catholic Emancipation.* An engraving of a funeral parade in his honor in New York City

adorned the walls of many Irish immigrant homes across America.

The hero adopted by Young Ireland, Theobald Wolf Tone, was a Dublin Protestant who is now considered the father of Irish Nationalism. In 1798, he organized the Society of United Irishmen, and inspired Henry Joy McCracken to lead a rebellion of some ten thousand northern Protestants against British rule. Supported by an abortive invasion from France, and by the "Defenders" or the "Catholic Arm," who rose in rebellion with him in County Wexford, Tone's rebellion was suppressed. In the aftermath many thousands of people were forced into exile in the United States. Daniel O'Connell, then a young man, joined a unit of the British Yeomanry of Dublin and was prepared to fight Wolf Tone, the French, and the "Defenders" in order to preserve what he felt was the necessary link with England.

THE CATHOLIC IRISH
IN NEW YORK

The Irish began to receive a stormy reception in America as the swell of immigrants grew in the New York area in the late 1830s and early '40s due to the increasing lack of food in Ireland. Urban Americans were horrified by the poverty and lack of education in many of these people and their fears and resentment began to be focused on the Catholic faith of the newcomers. For some reason German Catholics, almost equal in number to those from Ireland, did not meet the same prejudice, perhaps because the Protestant-Catholic conflict in Germany was a purely internal issue, whereas in Ireland, it had long carried an underlying political connotation. Because of the English domination of Ireland, which was always resented, Catholics were potential rebels and were mistrusted. Irish Protestants were more likely to be loyal to English rule. The United States, despite its own revolution from England less than a century earlier, still largely maintained the attitudes of its Anglo-Saxon Protestant heritage.

As what were characterized as "hoards" of Irish began to invade the eastern seaboard, the Native American Party, later to be known as the Know-Nothing Party, was founded in 1845. Known clandestinely as the Order of the Star Spangled Banner, the group was pledged to fight the menace posed by Catholicism to American ideals. Among other things Catholics provoked Protestant resistance by campaigning for public funds for parochial schools, asserting that the Protestant Bible was required public-school reading material. Reactions to Catholicism in many instances went beyond simple political opposition and degenerated into violence: Catholic churches and convents were burned. In many instances, the leading advocates of this violence were Protestant Irishmen, carrying the prejudice of the old country to the United States.

The violence reached its peak in Philadelphia in 1844 when twenty people were killed, hundreds more were wounded, and three Catholic churches were burned to the ground. One of Currier and Ives's competitors, J. L. Magee, published a print entitled *Death of George Shifler,* picturing a victim of the riot in Philadelphia. The print shows a dying Shifler (an Irish Protestant) wrapped in an American flag claiming that he was murdered by enemies of the United States, in other words, Catholics.

Currier and Ives avoided such anti-Irish lithographs, preferring instead to publish scenes of Irish life and history and portraits of respected figures such as Cardinal Hughes, Cardinal McCloskey, and views of Saint Patrick's Cathedral. In later years, Currier and Ives would publish hundreds of religious prints having no particular relation to Ireland or the Irish but clearly targeted to the Catholic population. Currier and Ives avoided prints dealing with the controversy between religious groups and the issue of Catholic education, which continued as a source for the publishing of anti-Catholic prints and news accounts for perhaps a hundred years and remains a political issue.

The political opposition to Catholics on the national level continued, although it finally abated with the coming of a more contentious issue to the surface in the late 1850s, that of slavery. The issue of slavery, of course, led to the Civil War, whereas the Protestant-Catholic contention dissolved into an undercurrent, which finally resolved itself with the election of John F. Kennedy to the presidency in 1960.

Opposite:
ARCHBISHOP JOHN HUGHES

JOHN HUGHES
FIRST ARCHBISHOP OF NEW YORK

At a mass meeting of Irish-Americans in New York in the early 1850s speaker after speaker got up and addressed the crowd, urging them to go west, to leave the slums and the decaying conditions in which they lived and find new and better lives elsewhere in this vast country. A man in old tattered clothing rose from the audience to oppose the speakers, claiming that what they meant was, "You go and we stay."

The crowd swung to the sentiment of the stranger, who then revealed his identity as Archbishop John Hughes of Saint Patrick's Cathedral. Why did Hughes speak up in this way? He may have wanted to protect the crowd's Catholicism, because many Irish who went west in the early days had to join a Protestant denomination if they wanted any spiritual comfort. In many areas Catholic churches were few and far between. Whatever his motivation, Hughes's advice worked well in the long run. As the numbers of Irish in New York increased, they eventually gained better jobs, better living conditions, and a good deal of control at City Hall, enjoying all the patronage that went with it.

John Hughes came to America with his parents from County Tyrone in 1817. He was ordained in 1825 and served as a parish priest in Philadelphia before being consecrated Archbishop of New York in 1838 in a church called Saint Patrick's Cathedral. This cathedral, now called Old Saint Patrick's, was founded by a German Jesuit, Anthony Kohlmann, and was built between 1809 and 1815 in what was then a beautiful suburb of New York City, but which today is the corner of Mott and Prince streets in the Bowery. The cathedral was to serve the needs of a growing Catholic community composed predominantly of people of Irish and German extraction.

In the manner of Protestant denominations, Old Saint Patrick's had a Board of Trustees that was elected by the laity. This board controlled finances, had the power to dismiss the pastor, and could make appointments to the school. This system was introduced in the hope that such local control would make a Catholic church, with its headquarters in Rome, seem less threatening to the New York Protestant community.

Archbishop Hughes, who became known as Dagger John, was a tough customer. He was not long in getting control of the church, although he had to go to the congregation to evict the established board of trustees. Hughes saw to the election of a subservient one. His main battles, however, were against the opposition of an established Protestant community. The founding fathers had enshrined freedom of religion in the Bill of Rights, but not all of their descendants were happy with the expanding Catholic presence in major American cities. As New York grew after the departure of the British in 1783 from a city of approximately 10,000 residents to one of 300,000 in 1840, a substantial percentage of the newcomers were Catholic Irish and German immigrants. By 1855, the city had a population of 600,000 and over 50 per cent were immigrants, including some 175,000 Irish and 95,000 Germans. With Hughes as their leader they were a formidable force.

Orangemen (Protestant Irishmen) fighting a rearguard Battle of the Boyne with some help from other local Protestants, attacked Catholics in Greenwich Village in 1824. When they planned to sack Old Saint Patrick's in 1835, the Irish came out in thousands and defended the cathedral. The Native American Democratic Association had been formed that year to oppose Catholism, pauperism, immigration, and foreign influence in public office. This was followed by the formation in 1845 of the Native American Party, which violently opposed the Irish immigrants and was determined to resist their advancement into the mainstream of American life. Its members were sworn to secrecy; when asked about their activities, their proper reply was, "I know nothing." This proved to be the opening that the Irish needed: being quick of wit, they labeled the group the Know-Nothing Party.

Though the Know-Nothings succeeded in attracting many prominent and respected men to their cause, they were doomed to failure. Early counterattacks by Bishop Hughes, great sacrifices made by the Irish in the Civil War, and the growing political power of an expanding Catholic population, all led to the eventual acceptance of Irish Catholics into American society.

Hughes was the type of Irish Catholic whose primary allegiance was to the pope and the supremacy of the church. He hated Irish Republicanism and the uncontrolled expressions of freedom and liberty that were sweeping Europe at that time and were also very popular with his own flock. However, there were times when he had to bend. One occasion was when the famous Irish rebel Terrence Bellow McManus died in San Francisco in 1861. His body was brought across country on the way to be buried in Ireland, and a solem High Mass and requiem was celebrated at Saint Patrick's Cathedral. Archibishop Hughes preached a sermon upholding the right of the oppressed to struggle for liberation. He said that McManus had sacrified his prospects in life and even life itself for the freedom of a country that he had loved so well and which he knew had been oppressed for centuries.

By siding with the Irish in their radical political views when necessary and by serving the religious needs of all Catholics, Hughes developed for the Archdiocese of New York a growing political power and influence.

During the Civil War, in 1863, a proposed law permitting a rich man to buy out of the draft for three hundred dollars outraged the Irish population's sense of justice and fair play. In the massive riots that followed, they turned against a scapegoat, the black population. This is not something the Irish are proud of today: hundreds of people, including blacks, police, and government officials as well as Irish rioters, were killed. Archbishop Hughes was called upon by New York's governor, Horatio Seymour, to use his influence to stop the disorders. Though sick and infirm Dagger John did just that. He called a meeting and addressed five thousand people in front of his home at 36th Street and Madison Avenue, exorting them to respect law and order. Ashamed of their conduct, the crowd obeyed him.

By this time, Hughes had set his sights beyond Saint Patrick's to a new cathedral in the suburbs—at 51st Street and Fifth Avenue—which would become part of the expanding city. He died, however, in 1864 without seeing his dream fulfilled. When the new cathedral was finally built, Old Saint Patrick's would continue to administer its own parish as a neighborhood church. The old structure is still there as an active church and school despite the derelicts sleeping on its entrance steps in a blighted neighborhood.

The Irish are long gone uptown and into the suburbs. They climbed the ladder of success, leaving Old Saint Pat's and Dagger John largely forgotten.

What Clonmacnoise was to ancient Ireland, the new Saint Patrick's Cathedral is to the CatholicIrish of America, the spiritual center of their faith. Saints Peter and Paul greet you at the entrance, but it is the statue of Saint Patrick that occupies the inner sanctum directly opposite the pulpit. The cathedral distributes a small pamphlet to the public containing the following brief history: "Saint Patrick's was the dream of John Hughes, the first Archbishop of New York. James Renwick, the noted mid-19th century architect, crystallized that dream in blueprints of a great Gothic cathedral. The foundations had only just been laid when tragedy struck this nation—the horror of the Civil War. Weeds grew wild over what should have been a testimony to man's love, and not until fourteen years after the end of the Civil War was the Cathedral opened, completed under the direction of John Cardinal McCloskey. It was not in its present completed form (the spires were not lifted until about ten years later and the Lady Chapel was added at the turn of the century), but it was true to the traditional Gothic style, common in European churches built from the thirteenth to the fifteenth centuries . . . and although it reminds some of other cathedrals, Cologne and Rheims for instance, it has always been original and distinctive."

Like its predecesor, Old Saint Patrick's, this cathedral is also run by a board of trustees. Its total cost of $2.5 million was raised in part through assessments to the existing parishes of the archdiocese. In addition, various committees raised substantial sums both from ordinary hard working women and men as well as from Irish Catholics who had made it big in the New World, including a $200,000 donation from a Mrs. Eugene Kelly. Some critics called it a monument to the egotism of the New York Irish. It was Dagger John's desire that the new cathedral should be one "of suitable magnificence" for the growing Catholic population of New York and the United States and he named it unashamedly for the great and glorious Apostle of Ireland, Saint Patrick.

Today the regular parishioners of Saint Patrick's Cathedral number only about three hundred, but the cathedral serves the needs of a huge tourist population each weekend, with up to four thousand people attending Mass on Sundays. It is still a seat of controversy, with its guiding cardinals over the years acting as lightning rods for a range of issues.

Most in line with the spirit of Dagger John, perhaps, is the present Cardinal O'Connor who is unyielding in upholding traditional Catholic views, yet mindful of the continued influence of the Irish in liberal matters. He has, for example, supported imprisoned IRA man Joseph Doherty in his long fight for political asylum in America and has called for a British withdrawal from Northern Ireland, an issue which had embarrassed his predecessors into silence. A recent news item in the *Irish Voice* newspaper noted that due to threats against the cathedral, Cardinal O'Connor had issued a call to the Irish-American community to be ready to defend their cathedral again as they had done with Old Saint Pat's 160 years ago.

ARCHBISHOP JOHN MCCLOSKEY

LIFE IN THE "AULD" COUNTRY

The life that the early immigrants escaped was one of grinding poverty, but in the relative prosperity of the New World they delighted in remembering good times in Ireland. The Currier and Ives prints perpetuate the image of the Irish peasant as optimistic and fun-loving, though with a violent streak never far from the surface. Smoking, drinking, courting, dancing, and racing are all portrayed in these priceless images of life in mid-nineteenth-century Ireland.

It seems that even when they gathered together to pray, as in *A Pattern in Connemara*, country folk saw the day dissolve into riotous fun and rough athletic games. *Paddy and the Pigs* is a curiously mixed scene of poverty, coy storytelling, and comraderie. *"Auld Times" at Donnybrook Fair* emphasizes music, dancing, and the capacity of both young and old to have fun together, even though alcohol and violence may lurk in the background. The same theme is present in *"Jantin Car,"* except that the pipe replaces the bottle of liquor. The portraits of the ladies suggest a more elegant style of life, but the faces are inescapably those of Irish peasant girls.

The Irishman's way of life in America, with its idealized but beautiful memories of the homeland, found Paddy now busy making bricks or laying railroad tracks, but able to offer his family food on the table and the prospect of a better future for his children. He could still look back whimsically and almost wish he had never left.

"AULD TIMES" AT DONNYBROOK FAIR

Before the "auld times" were ended by the British in 1854, the name of this fair had worked its way into the language. It was a real donnybrook, a brawl, yes. But it was fun and nobody really got hurt, at least not that badly.

The fair was established in 1204 by King John of England in what is today a residential district of Dublin, three miles southeast of the center of the city on the main road to the seaside resort of Bray. It became famous for its wild merrymaking. Thousands of people came together and set up hundreds of tents adorned with flags or scraps of color that denoted the origin of its occupants. Rope dancers and jugglers dressed in colorful finery performed on rough wooden stages. They mesmerized the crowds with their grimacing and dancing until both performer and audience were exhausted. There was eating, drinking, smoking, card playing, love-making, quarreling, and fighting. The crowds of men and women as well as old people and youngsters all had a good time without fear or care. The spirited music and dancing is well captured by this wonderful Currier and Ives print. And this song by an anonymous author gives us more:

To Donnybrook steer, all you sons of Parnassus
Poor painters, poor poets, poor newsmen, and knaves
To see what the fun is that all fun surpasses,
The sorrow and sadness of green Eirn's slaves
Old Donnybrook Jewel full of mirth as you quiver,
Where all flock from Dublin to gape and to stare
At two elegant bridges without e're a river,
So success to the humours of Donnybrook Fair!
There Tinkers and Nailers and Beggers and Tailors
and singers of ballad and girls of the sieve
with Barrack Street Rangers, the known ones and strangers
And many that no one can tell how they live,
These are horsemen and walkers and likewise fruit-hawkers
and swindlers the devil himself that would dare
With pipers and fiddlers and dandies and diddlers
All meet in the humours of Donnybrook Fair.
'Tis there are dogs dancing and wild beasts a-prancing
With neat bits of painting in red, yellow and gold
Toss-players and scramblers and showmen and gamblers,
Pickpockets in plenty, both of young and of old;
There are brewers and bakers and jolly shoemakers
With butchers and porters and men that cut hair,
There are mountebanks grinning while others are sinning
To keep of the humours of Donnybrook Fair.
Brisk lads and young lasses can there fill their glasses
With whiskey and send a full bumper around,
Jig it off in a tent till their money's all spent
And spin like a top till they rest on the ground.
Oh Donnybrook capers to sweet catguts scrapers
They bother the vapours and drive away care,
And what is more glorious, there's naught more uproarious
Huzza the humours of Donnybrook Fair!

The musical instrument shown in the print is the Uillean pipe. The bagpipe was outlawed in Ireland by the British, probably because of its association with military marching bands. With the Uillean pipes, a wind instrument, the moving air is produced by the player squeezing a bag held under the arm, as opposed to blowing into it. The device became popular because of the law forbidding bagpipes. In modern times the bagpipes have regained their primacy, but Uillean pipes are still played by traditional Irish musicians.

Above: "AULD TIMES" AT DONNYBROOK FAIR

Next pages: PADDY MURPHY'S "JANTIN CAR"

The title of the Currier and Ives print tries to give the word "jaunting" in an Irish accent. The words of the song below, written and composed by Valentine Vousten in New York in 1855, make no such pretense.

Do you want a car Your Honor? Och! Sure that's the
    one for you,
It's an outside Irish Jaunting Car, just painted green
    and blue
It belongs to Paddy Murphy* and you'll have to
    travel far
To find a better driver of an Irish Jaunting Car,
The fare is 15 pence but as the distance isn't far,
I'll just say one and three pence ma'am so jump up
    on the car.

If you want to drive round Dublin, sure you'll find
    me on the stand;
I'll take you to Raheny, to pick up cockles on the
    strand,

To the Phoenix Park to Nancy Hands, the Monument,
    and then
I'll take you to the Strawberry Beds and back to town
    again
Get some bread and beef and porter and some
    whiskey in a jar
That's the way to take your pleasure on an Irish
    Jaunting Car.

Oh, then, if that car should speak, Sir, sure a moral
    'twould disclose
It has carried Whigs and Tories, Repealers and their
    foes;
Yet it looks well by obliging all—and keeps me better
    far,
with my whip, my pipe, my pony and my Irish Jaunt-
    ing Car.
So if you want to hire me, call into Mr. Mahar,
And he'll send for Paddy Murphy, and his Irish
    Jaunting Car.

ENCORE VERSES

Well, I see you're fond of driving
But of course I can't complain
When you're inclined to give me
    double fare
and hire me out again;
But the pony's getting tired, for tonight
    he's travel'd far,
Yet I know that he's a good one, so I'll
    just Re-verse the car.

It's an antique Irish vehicle, us'd in
    memory of the way
That Erin's war like sons behaved in
    many a bygone fray,
When back to back they stood and
    fought, nor heeded wound or scar,
As now its back to back they sit upon
    the Jaunting Car
And should a jealous thought presume
    their happiness to mar,
They'll take and drown' it in the well
    of th' Irish Jaunting Car

Its Cupid's own conveyance, in the
    well amongst the hay,
The little rouge conceals himself, to
    hear what sweethearts say
and oh! the blarny that he hears, sure
    my tongue can't repeat,
It's enough to smash the car and knock
    the driver from his seat;
'twould change the war-like notions of
    the great big Russian Czar,
If he heard the conversation on an
    Irish Jaunting Car.

*Larry Doolan, in the original version

PADDY AND THE PIGS

Did you ever go into an Irishmen's shanty?
Ah! there boys you'll find the whiskey so plenty
With a pipe in his mouth there sits Paddy so free
No King in his palace is prouder than he.

There's a three legged stool and a table to match,
And the door of the shanty is locked with a latch;
There is a neat feather mattress all bursting with straw,
For the want of a Bedstead, it lies on the floor.

There's a neat little Bureau without paint or gilt,
Made of boards that was left when the shanty was built,
And a three cornered mirror that hangs on the wall,
But divil a picture's been in it at all.

It has three rooms in one; Kitchen, bedroom and hall,
And his chest, it is three wooden pegs on the wall,
He's two suits of old clothes, tis a wardrobe complete
One to wear in the shanty, the same in the street.

He's a pig in the sty, and a cow in the stable
And feeds them on scraps, that's left from the table
They get sick if confined, so they roam at their ease,
And go into the shanty whenever they please.

There is one who partakes of his sorrows and joys,
Who attends to the shanty, the girls and the boys;
The brats he thinks more of, than gold that's refined,
But biddy's the jewel that's set in his mind.

From the song "The Irishmen's Shanty" by Henry Tucker, New York, 1859

A Pattern in Connemara

Saint Patrick climbed Maumturk Mountain and came to the Maumean Pass and looked out across the wilderness to the "Twelve Bens" beyond. But feeling the power of the ancient religion and the spirit of Tuatha De Danann, that mystical but vanquished race that had inhabited Ireland before the Celts, he went no further and so failed to enter what subsequently became known as the Kingdom of Connemara.

For fifteen hundred years, right up to the 1970s, crowds of people came to this place to pray. The gatherings were known as "patterns," which came from the Gaelic word *patrun* (as in patron saint). Each saint had a pattern day.

As time went by, the prayers became secondary, something to be hurried through, and the celebration took on the attributes of the Donnybrook Fair, with music, drinking, merrymaking, and fighting with shillelaghs the main attractions. (Fighting with shillelaghs was a form of mock combat with sticks, in which one parish put up a combatant against another. But nobody got hurt and there were no hard feelings once the game was over.)

The Currier and Ives print shows the rock formation atop the mountain in the form of a chapel. Nearby is a holy well and a large mound of stones known as Saint Patrick's bed, where the saint is believed to have rested.

THE ROSE OF KILLARNEY

THE PRIDE OF KILDARE.

NEW YORK, PUBLISHED BY CURRIER & IVES, 125 NASSAU ST.

THE IRISH BEAUTY.

PUBLISHED BY CURRIER & IVES, 152 NASSAU ST. NEW YORK.

THE PRIDE OF KILDARE

County Kildare in central Ireland did not receive much attention from Currier and Ives. Part of the central plain, it features little scenic beauty. One notable sight, however, is the Curragh Racetrack, six miles long and two miles wide, which has existed in some form since ancient times, and which today hosts the finest racehorses in the world. As the print shows, if the land in Kildare lacked beauty, its women certainly did not.

THE IRISH BEAUTY

When Irishmen abroad joined the armies of other nations, they tended to idealize the girls back home. A popular song with the Irish brigades in the Civil War was "The Girl I Left Behind Me."

The dames of France are fond and free,
and Flemish lips are willing,
and soft the maids of Italy, and Spanish eyes are thrilling,
still, though I bask beneath their smile,
their charms fail to bind me,
and my heart falls back to Erin's Isle
to the girl I left behind me.
She says "my own dear love come home,
my friends are rich and many
or else, abroad with you I'll roam, a soldier stout as any;
if you'll not come, nor let me go,
I'll think you have resign'd me,"
My heart nigh broke when I answered "No"
to the girl I left behind me.

Anonymous

61

IRELAND'S FIGHT
FOR FREEDOM
(AT HOME AND ABROAD)

The year 1848 saw the spread of revolution throughout western Europe as the peace achieved by the Battle of Waterloo began to fall apart. Ireland was no exception, though there revolution was on a tiny scale, beginning and ending in a minor skirmish: one hundred rebels struggled against forty constabularies at a farmhouse in County Tipperary. The revolutionaries were called Young Ireland, a force composed mostly of writers. There were no generals and few weapons. The ill-equipped soldiers had empty stomachs due to the great famine that had begun in the spring of 1847. Defeated easily, the leaders of Young Ireland were sentenced to death, but their sentences were later commuted by Queen Victoria and they were sent into exile in Van Diemen's land, which became the Australian state of Tasmania. Most escaped and came to America.

The arrival of these leaders in America occurred in tandem with massive emigration from Ireland that was due to the famine. It shifted the focus of the campaign for Irish freedom to the United States. The hundreds of thousands of penniless peasants then arriving in America identified with the Young Ireland leaders. Both, after all, had been exiled from their homes, some for their political actions, and most because of eviction by their English landlords. The combination of these two parallel events gave focus to a powerful resentment, and many immigrants dreamed of going back to help Ireland gain its independence.

This emotional fervor was harvested by both sides in the Civil War, but especially in the North. Some Young Ireland leaders were transformed into Union officers. They urged immigrants to join up and gain the battle experience they would need to fight the English. An early opportunity to do this might even have been had if the Union had gone to war with England over its support of the South. When the war was over and that dream faltered some veterans, now calling themselves the Irish Republican Army, mounted an attack on Canada, the nearest and most vulnerable outpost of the British Empire. At the same time, they sent hundreds of now-seasoned combat veterans to Ireland to lead the Fenian Rebellion there. All military efforts failed, however, though there was a serious attempt to gain by peaceful means the freedom that Daniel O'Connell sought before the famine internationalized the struggle. With the rise of Charles Stewart Parnell, whose roots were in both America and Ireland, the focus of the struggle once more returned to home, and efforts from the American side of the Atlantic were reduced to financial and political support.

Currier and Ives captured this amazing story with prints of the Young Ireland movement, portraits of popular Irish heroes of the Civil War, and scenes of the Fenian struggle and the later parliamentary battles of Parnell. The struggle for Irish freedom outlasted Currier and Ives and their contemporary prints have long since become history. But the Irish efforts for freedom have continued.

Opposite:
JOHN MITCHEL

John Mitchel
The First Martyr of Ireland in Her Revolution of 1848

At the close of the Civil War, Confederate President Jefferson Davis, a public enemy of the United States of America, was imprisoned at Fortress Monroe on Chesapeake Bay. In the same prison, locked in a small vaulted room lighted only by a porthole, was John Mitchel, public enemy number two of the United States.

Mitchel, the publisher of a pre–Civil War paper called *The Southern Citizen*, had a provocative pen that cut to the heart of every truth and later became a weapon that spewed out venom as chief apologist for the South and its institution of slavery. Now, as he sat in prison on the orders of General Grant for his recent writings in the *New York Daily News*, he reflected on his own situation, which had come full circle. At Fortress Monroe he would remain defiant by writing: "it is true, the English government took care to have a Special Act of Parliament passed for my incarceration; but our Yankees disdain in these days to make any pretense of law at all; they simply seize upon those who are inconvenient and suppress the delinquents." The slavery issue had come and gone, but Mitchel's magnificent journal from jail remains an enduring example of the human spirit's struggle against colonialism and tyranny.

Mitchel's enemies in Britain, who had also supported the South, could not refrain from taunting him in his present plight. They said he was a rebel by nature and a lawbreaker by instinct. He was in fact a man of strong convictions without any fear, and he took on almost single-handedly the entire British administration in Ireland.

John Mitchel, son of a Protestant minister, was convicted in Dublin on May 25, 1848, for the crime of treason. His crime consisted of being publisher and editor of the newspaper *United Irishman,* which advocated rebellion against English rule. The sentence was fourteen years in an overseas penal colony. After being sentenced, Mitchel himself summed it up:

> The law has done its part, and the Queen of England, her crown and government in Ireland, are now secure, pursuant to Act of Parliament. I have done my part also. Three months ago I promised Lord Clarendon and his Government, who hold this country for the English, that I would provoke him into his courts of justice, as places of this kind are called, and that I would force him, publicly and notoriously, to pack a jury against me to convict me, or else that I would walk a free man out of this Court, and provoke him to a contest in another field. My Lords, I know I was setting my life on that cast; but I knew that, in either event,

> victory should be with me; and it is with me. Neither the jury nor the Judges, nor any other man in this Court presumes to imagine that it is a criminal who stands in this dock. [Murmurs of applause which the police endeavored to repress.] I have shown what the law is made of in Ireland. I have shown that Her Majesty's government sustains itself in Ireland by packed juries, by partisan judges, by perjured sheriffs.

John Mitchel's real crime, in the eyes of historians, was that this persuasive Northern Ireland Protestant gentleman, along with Thomas Davis and other Protestants who had joined with Catholics to form a movement called Young Ireland, had a real chance of persuading the Protestants and Catholics of Ireland to unite for freedom. With Mitchel convicted, exiled abroad for fourteen years, and his paper suppressed, the religious division was maintained and the British presence in Ireland secured.

The Currier and Ives print shows John Mitchel seated pensively with his newspaper in his right hand, glancing at the convict ship in the bay that would transport him eventually to Van Diemen's Land while his wife and children remained in Ireland. First, however, he was removed in chains to Spike Island Prison in the Cove of Cork. From there on June 1, 1848, he was transported to Bermuda on the *Scourge*, a long, low, rakish-looking steamer with black hull and two funnels.

In Bermuda, Mitchel was held on a ship called the *Dromedary* off an island called, of all things, Ireland. He remained there for almost a year, until told that he was to be transported to Cape Town, South Africa, where the British were planning to establish a new penal colony. He then sailed on the convict ship *Neptune*. While at sea Mitchel described its occupants in his diary:

> There are nearly 200 Irish amongst these prisoners, the famine-struck Irish of the Special Commission; many who have not a word of English, and most of them so shattered in constitution by mere hunger and hardship that all the deaths amongst the prisoners, ever since we embarked, have been Irish. What a fate! What a dreary doom has been spun and woven for you, my countrymen! They were born, these men, to a heritage of unquenched hunger, amongst the teaming plenty of their motherland, hunted like noxious beasts from all shelter on her hospitable bosom, driven to stay their gnawing enemy with what certain

respectable fed men call their 'property'. And so now, they are traversing the deep under bayonet points, to be shot out like rubbish on a bare foreign strand, and told to seek their fortune there amongst a people whose very language they know not. Many of them, I believe, being without families, are glad of this escape, as they might be glad of any escape from the circle of hunters that chased them for life at home. But then there are many others (boys from twelve to seventeen years of age, and some of them very handsome boys, with fine open countenances, and a laugh so clear and ringing) whom it is a real pain to look upon. They hardly know what troops of fell foes, with quivers full of arrows, are hunting for their young souls and bodies; they hardly know, and—so much the poor pity for them—hardly feel it."

After three months at sea in poor sailing conditions they stopped at Pernambuco, Brazil where they loaded supplies, arriving off the Cape five months after leaving Bermuda. The settlers of the Cape were unhappy with the prospect of a penal colony being established there and were close to revolt, so that when the *Neptune* arrived it was unable to put its human cargo ashore. Mitchel took the side of the South Africans in his Journal:

> the Carthaginian government [Mitchel's name for the English] claim to be entitled to palm some of their convict rascality upon the Cape, because they supplied troops to save the Cape from Caffirs —but, say these newspapers, you did this to uphold Carthaginian supremacy in Southern Africa, not to protect our households—and though it were not so, still we say, take your troops, take your ships: we will defend ourselves from the Caffirs; at the very worst we prefer Caffirs to convicts.

While off South Africa, Mitchel learned that a week before his arrival another convict ship called the *Swift* touched there and took on provisions on her way to Sydney. William Smith O'Brien, Thomas Francis Meagher, Patrick O'Donohue, and Terence McManus were on board. The knowledge that three other convict ships were at sea, including one holding his friends John Martin and Kevin O'Doherty, caused him to comment that "on Britain's convict-ships, the sun never sets." After a standoff at the Cape lasting four months, the British finally yielded and the *Neptune* moved on to Van Diemen's Land.

This large island off southeastern Australia, now called Tasmania, was the most famous of all British penal colonies for the Irish. They arrived at Hobart Town, Van Diemen's Land, eleven months after leaving Bermuda. In compensation for the hardships of their long voyage and

detention, all the prisoners received "her Gracious Majesty's Conditional Pardon . . . except the Prisoner Mitchel." On arrival at the island on April 7, 1850, however, he was given a form of parole, in which he was confined to a geographical area after signing a promise not to escape.

Life was not unpleasant in this beautiful place, with its Avoca Valley and River Shannon named after the old country. Here, thousands of political convicts from Ireland, together with run-of-the-mill thieves and prostitutes from the London pavements, settled down to be small farmers, tradespeople, servants, or even policemen. Mitchel reported monthly to the local police station. In time, his wife and children joined him in Van Diemen's Land. There was, of course, the inevitable reunion deep in the mountains with his compatriots Meagher, McManus, and O'Brien. There they laughed and cried and talked about their followers in the Irish communities of the United States, and of their trials and tribulations. They realized that to escape would be easy, since they swam in a sea of friendly ex-convicts united against the authorities. Mitchel, however, was determined to escape honorably. One day, after three years on the island, he entered a police station, announced that he no longer accepted the terms of his parole, and rushed out and jumped on his horse. With the police chasing him, he disappeared into the forest.

> We gave the bridle-rein a shake;
> said adieu for ever more, my dear;
> and adieu for ever more!

Mitchel's escape was aided by Patrick Joseph Smyth, who had come from a New York Irish Society with money to secure passage to the United States. (Meagher had gone there after escaping the previous year.) After six weeks on the run in Van Diemen's Land, Mitchel, disguised as a priest, booked passage on the brig *Emma* bound for California. His wife and family had already boarded the same boat. On arrival in San Francisco he was given a tumultuous welcome and was the toast of the city. New York, however, was his ultimate destination, and he traveled there by way of Panama. His mother, who had heard of his escape from Van Diemen's Land, had travelled from Ireland to New York and bought a house in Brooklyn. When John arrived, he was greeted on the dock by Meagher and at his mother's house he found his own name on the door. He had circumnavigated the globe.

New York was a replay of San Francisco; banquets, receptions, and honors were lavished on him. He quickly joined the political scene by publishing a paper called *The Citizen*. Although it was an initial success, the paper would soon face strong opposition, for its anticlerical bent put Mitchel in conflict with Archbishop Hughes of Saint Patrick's Cathedral. Mitchel also published a defense of slavery, which drew the ire of the Rev. Henry Ward Beecher and the abolitionists, whom he viewed as hypocrites. Beecher, however, painted Mitchel as the hypocrite, saying that he could not see how a man who was a champion of freedom in Ireland could support slavery in America. Many Irish immigrants did not understand it either and the paper lost support. For his part, Mitchel

> began to understand fully, what I had partly suspected before, that dwelling on the land of the United States there are two na-tions, not one only; and that the two are separated not more sharply than a geographical line by their institutions, habits, industrial requirements, and political principles. There is a northern nation and a southern, and possibly it may come to this, that they must either peacefully separate, dividing the continent between them, or else the one must conquer the other. For so far, I do not hope it will come to this; but, if it do, I think all my sympathies would be with the south.

Widely denounced, Mitchel departed for Knoxville, Tennessee. There, he founded *The Southern Citizen*, which became the voice and conscience of the Southern states. For Mitchel, however, the Southern cause remained a secondary one, and when the prospect of war developed between France and England in 1859, he abandoned *The Southern Citizen* and went to Paris to see if there might be an opportunity for Ireland in such a conflict. He determined that there was none and returned to the United States in 1862 with the Civil War in full swing.

Mitchel's family, now grown to six children, included three sons who were fighting for the Confederacy. John Jr., a hero to the South, was commanding officer of Fort Sumter, and was killed on July 20, 1864, by a shell fragment. Willie was killed as part of Pickett's Charge on Cemetery Ridge at the Battle of Gettysburg on July 4, 1863. James, his only surviving son, was chief of staff to General Gordon at the Battle of Chancellorsville. Mitchel's wife was in Ireland at the outbreak of the war. Fearful for her three sons in America, she collected supplies for them and booked passage aboard a blockade runner, the *Vesta*, to reach the Confederacy. The saga of the *Vesta* was a strange one. After having successfully run the blockade and evaded eight pursuing ships, the *Vesta*'s captain got drunk, deposited Mrs. Mitchel on the banks of the Cape Fear River, and burned the ship with all its cargo.

When the war was over, for his role in the South Mitchel was imprisoned. The Civil War had divided the nation, but the Irish who had taken different sides quickly reunited, and a delegation sent to President Johnson brought John Mitchel's freedom from Fortress Monroe. He returned to New York, though in failing health. Ten years later, in February 1875, he returned to Ireland and stood for election with the Home Rule Party in County Tipperary. "I shall immediately present myself to you in person, and ask Tipperary to confer upon me the highest honor that I can conceive awarded to mortal man—that of being the representative of the premier county." The British prime minister, Benjamin Disraeli, declared Mitchel a felon and voided the election, but the voters returned him again with an even larger majority. Mitchel refused to take his seat in the British parliament, however, as he had promised the people of Tipperary that he would represent them otherwise. Before he could explain what he meant, his health declined dramatically and he died shortly thereafter.

In 1918, in the last election ever held for all of Ireland, the Sein Fein Party won 80 percent of the Irish seats in the British parliament and every elected member refused to take his seat in the House of Commons in London in accordance with the principles established by John Mitchel. They met, instead, as a separate Irish parliament in Dublin. The results of the 1918 election were also suppressed, and the English refusal to accept the will of the majority of the Irish people is the cause of continuing strife in Ireland.

SIGNAL FIRE ON SLIEVENAMON MOUNTAIN

From Carrick Streets to Shannon Shore
From Slievenamon to Ballinderry
From Longford Pass to Galtymore
Come, hear the vow of Tipperary

Too long we fought for Britain's cause
And of our blood were never chary;
she paid us back with tyrant laws,
and thinned the Homes of Tipperary

But nevermore, we'll win such thanks
here us, Oh God and Virgin Mary,
never to list in British ranks;
and that's the Vow of Tipperary

"The Vow of Tipperary" by Thomas Davis
(Poet of the Young Ireland Movement)

Slievenamon Mountain sits on the Plain of Feinhan along the valley of the Suir in that part of County Tipperary that borders on County Waterford to the south and Kilkenny to the east. The name Slievenamon comes from the Gaelic *sliabh-na-mBan Bh-Fionn* or the Mountain of the Fair Women. The mountain rises nearly 2,400 feet. At the sum-

SIGNAL FIRE ON SLIEVENAMON MOUNTAIN

mit is the stone seat of Finn MacCumhall, chief of a band of idealistic warriors from the time of Christ who hunted the plains beneath. It was there in 1648 that Oliver Cromwell and his parliamentary army of Roundheads would exclaim on viewing the vast fertile plain extending before them that "this is a country worth fighting for." They had no way of knowing that some two hundred years later, in 1848, their descendants, who were now wealthy landlords in Tipperary, would be carefully chosen as a jury in an effort to stem the tide of rebellion let loose at the summit.

On Sunday July 16, 1848, Thomas Francis Meagher, just twenty-five years old, came to Slievenamon and climbed to the summit. Fifty thousand people from the surrounding counties also climbed the mountain that day to listen to Michael Doheny and Meagher. They spoke not only of the terrible potato blight that was causing famine throughout the land, but of the equally great hardship induced by the fact that the considerable recent harvests of grain were not made available to the people because they were shipped abroad for profit by the landlords.

Meagher, who had been arrested but was at liberty until his trial, spoke brave words to the crowd: "Men of Tipperary . . . I trust that they will find out that they have made a great mistake in arresting me . . . I am here not only to repent of nothing, but to dare them to do something worse . . . I felt that I lived in a land of slavery, and that if God gave me intellect, it ought to be employed for the country. It was with this feeling I joined the cause of Ireland at a moment when every nation wished to see her flag unfurled on these hills . . . the potato was smitten; but your fields waived with golden grain. It was not for you. To your lips it was forbidden fruit. The ships came and bore it away. . . . The fact is plain, that this land, which is yours by nature, and by God's gift, it is not yours by the law of the land."

Nearby, the large English garrisons stationed in the towns of Clonmel and Carrick-on-Suir watched the gathering with apprehension. All through the first half of 1848 signal fires on Slievenamon had roused the local population to the pitch of rebellion. The Currier and Ives print dramatizes the conspiratorial nature of these fires.

Nothing more dramatic than speeches took place on Slievenamon Mountain that night, and in the weeks that followed the embers of rebellion dimmed.

The union with England in 1800 had not improved in any way the plight of the rural population, whose standard of living shrank to a poverty level that may have been as low as any in the world. The census of 1841 had shown that half of Ireland's rural population lived in windowless, one-room mud cabins. Furniture of any kind was a luxury and beds were virtually nonexistent. Pigs slept with their owners and manure heaps were as likely to be inside as outside. For their cabins and small plots of land the peasants paid rents to the landed aristocracy. All the proceeds from the sale of grain and other crops went to pay this rent. What was left for the poor farmers to eat was the potato, and when blight attacked potato crops in 1845, 1846, and 1847 a terrible famine came over the land. Forced to continue to turn over their wheat or face eviction for nonpayment of rent, many faced starvation. Those who were evicted lived a miserable itinerant life on the roads, or found meager shelter in the mountains.

Meagher and the Young Ireland movement tried to stir the people to rebellion, but they were slow to rise in force because of their weakened condition, and also because many were desperate to hold onto what little economic resources they had and to save enough to escape to America.

A museum to commemmorate the one hundred fiftieth anniversary of the famine years has recently been opened at Strokestown, County Roscommon, on one of the estates that was notorious for evictions. Its primary purpose is to give the present generation some insight and appreciation of the sacrifices and horror suffered by those who were forced by circumstances to remain in Ireland during that terrible time.

In modern times, the words to another poem, *Slievenamon* by Charles Joseph Kickham, form an unofficial anthem of the men and women of Tipperary. The words are known to all and they have been sung as a cry of longing for the homeland for many years. They are sung today in a somewhat less political atmosphere, whenever those of Tipperary gather to play or watch the games of Gaelic football and hurling. Thus, historic Slievenamon continues to be more than just the name of a mountain. It brings images of victory, patriotism, and inspiration to the minds and hearts of Tipperary people and other Irish men and women who remember the events of 1848.

Print courtesy of The Library of Congress

WILLIAM SMITH O'BRIEN

In 1848 only one in a hundred of the population of Ireland had the right to vote. The voters were well-off property owners, influenced by landed gentry. The gentry had held most of the land of Ireland for centuries. The average Irish peasant was for the most part Catholic, owned no property, and had no say in his country's affairs. Every once in a while a member of the aristocracy took the radical view that he was an Irishman and not an Englishman. William Smith O'Brien was one of these rare individuals, and, like most of his class, he was a Protestant.

William Smith O'Brien was born in Dromoland Castle in County Clare. He claimed lineage from Brian Boru.

On April 10, 1848, William Smith O'Brien, delegate to the British parliament from Limerick, got up to speak in the House of Commons about the noble struggle for Irish independence. He was greeted by a chorus of laughter from the honorable members, but he never let derision affect him in any way. He was a gentleman to those who dealt with him, even when he turned from constitutional means to revolutionary tactics. His background, disposition, and sense of fair play made him, in a unique way, everybody's favorite revolutionary.

O'Brien had been converted to repeal of the union with Britain by the leadership of Daniel O'Connell. But, seeing that there was little hope for progress through the political process, he sided with Young Ireland and gained the friendship of the patriots who believed in physical force. Even those not fully committed to violence found his handling of the early stages of the rebellion acceptable. If William Smith O'Brien resorted to force there could be no other option. His conduct of the fight was as clean as if it were a sporting event.

An incident that illuminates his character involves the taking of a small police barracks at a place called Mullinahone in County Tipperary. O'Brien and two compatriots, James Stephens and Patrick O'Donohue, marched boldly into the barracks, surprised the sergeant at the main desk with their revolvers, and asked for his surrender. The sergeant suggested rather slyly that it would be terribly embarrassing for the six policemen present to surrender to just three men. He would be happy to surrender to an overwhelming force. This would enable the police to save face. O'Brien pondered the proposition, considered that the sergeant was also an Irishman and deserving of honor, and did just as he had been asked. He left and returned with fifteen armed men, but the police were long gone. In his own fashion O'Brien had taken the police barracks.

O'Brien was enormously popular. But the failure at the Widow McCormack's house (see page 70) enabled his enemies and especially the London *Times* to heap scorn on his efforts. The insurrection became, in their words, "the Cabbage Patch Rebellion," and they succeeded in

neutralizing his efforts with scorn and ridicule. More serious charges, however, came from the government. Treason was treason, after all, and with the other patriots of Clonmel, O'Brien was first condemned to death and later banished for life to Tasmania. In the end, his conduct of the revolution made it extremely difficult for the British authorities to execute him. He had played the game as a gentleman should.

Unlike other revolutionaries sentenced to Tasmania, O'Brien's attempt to escape to the United States failed. Rather than try again he decided to lobby for a pardon, which he ultimately received. He was permitted to return to Ireland in 1854. Thereafter, except for a visit to the United States in 1859, he lived a quiet life with his family, keeping up to date on the Irish struggle at a distance.

The leaders of the new revolutionary movements that were to follow O'Brien were conscious of the scorn that had been heaped on his methods. They vowed to be not so gentlemanly in such matters in the future.

The Currier and Ives print attempts to capture O'Brien as the man of letters he was, pictured in the beautiful setting of his home. But it also shows something of the dual aspect of his personality. In the background an Irish revolutionary band armed with pikes attacks the military.

ATTACK ON THE WIDOW
MCCORMACK'S HOUSE
ON BOULAGH COMMON,
JULY 29, 1848

ATTACK ON THE WIDOW MCCORMACK'S HOUSE ON BOULAGH COMMON, JULY 29, 1848

The attack on the Widow McCormack's house was vintage Irish insurrection at its farcical best. The print, one of the best that Currier and Ives ever published, captures the spirit of the moment even for someone who knows nothing about the incident. Clearly implied in it is the perception that the attacking force, with their variety of primitive weapons, are involved in an absurdity, a hopeless cause. In the aftermath of the attack its leaders were tried for treason and sentenced to death, although all sentences would later be commuted to exile in Van Diemen's Land.

The Ireland of 1848 was a desperate country. Devastated by years of famine and mass immigration, the population was depressed, broken, and hungry. The great Daniel O'Connell, who had earlier gained civil and political freedom for Catholics, but was now in the twilight of his career, had failed to persuade the government to provide food for the people and repeal the Union. Some dissatisfied members split from his Repeal movement to form Young Ireland, and were groping slowly toward revolution.

Some used the pen, others took to the pitchfork, and a few, embracing the spirit of revolution spreading on the continent of Europe, roamed the country hoping to find some trouble. Dublin was quiet, Kilkenny looked like a possibility, but the action—such as it was in 1848—took place in the county of Tipperary. There was conspiracy near Slievenamon and an encounter with the constabulary at Killenaul in the south, but with the forces of the government closing in on the leadership of the movement, the real action culminated in the siege of the Widow McCormack's house in the village of Ballingarry in South Tipperary. It happened under the leadership of a fine Protestant country gentleman named William Smith O'Brien.

The attack on the widow's house came about as a result of events which began on Saturday, July 29, 1848, when William Smith O'Brien and his compatriot, Terence McManus, with James Stephens, had assembled a force of one hundred men near the village of Ballingarry. As the print shows, they were armed with a few muskets, some pikes, and a few spears, pitchforks, spades, shovels, sticks, and stones.

This band of rebels discussed the possibility of linking up with similar forces at County Kilkenny to attack a police station at New Birmingham and perhaps escape toward Clonmel. Escape would not be easy, as the surrounding towns of Thurles, Kilkenny, and Cashel had large troop and police forces that were moving in on the insurgents.

A police inspector named Trant, intent on collecting a bounty that had been placed on the head of O'Brien, stole a march on the rest of the government forces and was hot on O'Brien's trail. With a force of forty constables all armed with rifles, they were more than a match for the Young Ireland army. O'Brien was alerted to Trant's approach and set up a barricade on the road from Ballingary. On approaching the barricade, Trant saw a large crowd of people. They were mostly spectators out for the show, but, thinking that there were thousands against him, Trant ran to a large stone farmhouse on a hill and barricaded himself and his troops. The house proved to be the residence of the Widow McCormack.

O'Brien's men surrounded the house and the leader himself walked up to the front door, shook hands with members of the constabulary, and asked them to surrender. He was uncomfortable with violence. Trant, however, refused, knowing that he had enough weapons and ammunition to hold out until help arrived. O'Brien immediately found himself under siege by the Widow McCormack, who had returned from a neighbor's house to find her five small children held hostage by the police. She called O'Brien every name in the book for placing her family in jeopardy. Crying and weeping, she pleaded with him to take his scoundrels and his revolution elsewhere.

While this was going on, young James Stephens, in a resourceful move, piled up some bales of hay against the back door in an effort to smoke out the garrison. When it was discovered that the attacking force did not have a match among them, he fired his pistol into the hay to get it started. O'Brien, however, swayed by the widow's concern for her children, made him remove the hay as soon as it began to burn. At the same time, a group of spectators, impatient with the pace of the rebellion, started throwing stones at the house, whereupon the police panicked and opened fire, killing one man and wounding a number of others. This immediately dampened the mood of the spectators and cured them of any fighting spirit. They left the scene as the battle raged.

The well-protected constabulary and their forty rifles were getting the better of the action when O'Brien went to a small lane behind the house and found that the local parish priest had convinced the bulk of his insurgents to abandon the rebellion and go home under the threat of eternal damnation. A disgusted O'Brien and a wounded Stephens escaped as strong military reinforcements moved in and scattered the remaining guerrilla band from the Widow McCormack's cabbage patch.

This would end O'Brien's and Young Ireland's involvement with rebellion. The resourceful Stephens used the excuse of his wounds to stage his own funeral, thus covering an ingenious escape. As if risen from the dead, he would return some twenty years later to organize the Fenians and lead a new generation in a new movement toward a future rebellion. Coincidentally, he would earn his own Currier and Ives print (See page 88).

Print courtesy of The Library of Congress

On July 1, 1867, the steamboat, *G. A. Thompson* was bound down river from Fort Benton, Montana, on the wide Missouri. It was dark and the river was high and swollen, with floods and muddy, turbulent undercurrents. Montana at that time was Indian Country. Desperadoes who had been loyal to the Confederacy roamed the region; the West was not quite won. Groups of professional politicians divided the spoils.

On board the *G. A. Thompson*, resting for the night, was the Secretary and Acting Governor of Montana, Thomas Francis Meagher, newly appointed by President Johnson and dedicated to a graft-free administration. Sometime after midnight the cry "man overboard" went up, and life rafts filled the muddy waters. To no avail. The acting governor was missing and presumed dead. Meagher, who had been in his time an orator, patriot, journalist, lawyer, explorer, soldier, and eventually an American politician, and who had been at the brink of death so many times, saw his luck finally run out at the relatively young age of forty-three. Years after the event, a man named Miller would confess that he murdered Meagher on a contract for hire. He later recanted and, since the death had been filed as an accident, there was no trial.

Meagher had been tried for treason some eighteen years before at Clonmel, County Tipperary. He had been sentenced to be hanged, drawn, and quartered for advocating rebellion in the year 1848, some months after his friend and compatriot John Mitchel had been sentenced to fourteen years penal servitude. Meagher's sentence, reflecting the enlightened hypocrisy of the times, was commuted to lifelong penal servitude in Van Diemen's Land. With the other "Patriots of Clonmel," he followed John Mitchel into exile to that prison island off Australia on board the man-of-war *Swift*. His description of the *Swift* in a letter to a friend, as the ship raced toward Australia, is sheer poetry. "I wish you could have seen her in a storm; at no other time did she look to such advantage. With a broken, scowling sky above her and a broken, scowling sea beneath, she gallantly dashed on. Glancing down the steepest valleys, she seemed to gather fresh force and bearing from the steepness of the fall; then breasting the highest waves, she would top them with a bound, and flinging their white crests and sparkling atoms right and left before her, spring further on—her beautiful light spars quivering like lances in the gale." Meagher also wrote a poetic description of the country that was to be his prison for life. "Nothing I have seen in other countries—Not Even My Own—equals the beauty, the glory of the scenery through which we glided up from Tasmans Head to Hobart Town."

Like John Mitchel, and in much the same manner, Meagher escaped from that beautiful prison in 1852, and sailed back around the Cape of Good Hope to Pernambuco, Brazil, and thence to New York, where he was hailed as a hero. Nobody since Lafayette had received such a tumultuous welcome as that accorded to Thomas Francis Meagher by the citizens of the United States.

In America, Meagher would use his great prestige to help his fellow countrymen pave the way for their acceptance into American society. In the four years that Meagher had spent in exile in Australia, millions of his fellow countrymen, fleeing the famine and for the most part unwanted in the New World, had crowded onto the American continent. Unlike Mitchel, who did not care what people thought of him and fought with just about every group, Meagher was a diplomat, very conscious of his image and his powers of persuasion. He saw it as a necessity and duty for himself and the Irish to pay America back for her generosity in accepting them.

Meagher would continue his career in America and go on to lead his fellow countrymen to glory as the Irish Brigade in the Civil War. Some historians have claimed that Meagher formed the brigade with the object of leading a trained army of invasion under American sponsorship back to Ireland after the war was over. It appears more likely that he used the emotions of his countrymen, their love and concern for the old country, and guided them to preserve the Union, perhaps also furthering his own career in the United States. In so doing, by oratory and example, he destroyed the Know-Nothing Party, as he climbed the ladder of success from captain to general to acting governor and paved the way for countless Irishmen who came after him, including Al Smith and John F. Kennedy.

After the Civil War, Meagher refused an invitation to be active with a movement called the Fenians, which sought to free the old country through a new armed struggle. With a home on Fifth Avenue, a beautiful American wife, and the opportunity to be Acting Governor of Montana, a new and unlimited future seemed to lie ahead of him. But it had not always been so.

Meagher had been born in County Waterford in 1823 to a well-to-do Catholic family. He attended the Jesuit School of Clongowes Wood, Dublin, and went on to the Stonyhurst school in England, where his eloquence and skill as a debater were duly noted. In 1843 he returned to Ireland and, with little knowledge of the history of his own country, was swept up by the ferment of Daniel O'Connell's movement for the repeal of the Act of Union with England. His eloquence and his enthusiasm for the cause ignited his countrymen, causing even the great

O'Connell to cheer and exclaim, "Bravo, Young Ireland," when he heard him speak.

Meagher came to Dublin and became fast friends with Thomas Davis, John Mitchel, William Smith O'Brien, and others who had formed the Young Ireland movement. His reputation as an orator drew thousands to their meetings, thus complementing the talents of the others. However, some six weeks after the forced exile of John Mitchel in 1848, Meagher was arrested and charged with sedition.

It didn't help him that some years previously he had given a famous speech, which caused him to be known as Meagher of the Sword:

Be it the defense, or be it in the assertion of a people's liberty, I hail the sword as a sacred weapon; and if, my Lord, it has sometimes taken the shape of a serpent, and reddened the shroud of the oppressor with too deep a dye, like the anointed rod of the High Priest, it has at other times, and as often, blossomed into celestial flowers to deck the freeman's brow. . . . Abhor the Sword, stigmatise the sword? No, my Lord, for at its blow, a giant nation started from the waters of the Atlantic, and by its redeeming magic, and in the quivering of its crimson light, the crippled Colony sprang into the attitude of a proud Republic—prosperous, limitless, and invincible!

It mattered not that the language of sedition in Ireland in 1848 was also the language of freedom. It was for this language that his trial took place. Released on his own recognizance, he took part in a council of war at Ballingarry with O'Brien, McManus, Stephens, and others, but he left to organize armed men at Slievenamon to attack the garrison at Clonmel and missed the action at the Widow McCormack's house the following day.

Before Meagher came to America, Currier and Ives followed his story and built his reputation in such prints as *Signal Fire on Slievenamon Mountain* and *Trial of the Irish Patriots at Clonmel*. Once Meagher came to the United States, Currier and Ives continued to follow his career and victories in the Civil War. After arriving in America in 1852, Meagher had immediately applied for citizenship. He made his living for a time as a journalist and orator (thousands of non-Irish came to hear his lectures about Australia), but there was no denying where he stood in the gathering storm that foreshadowed the coming of the Civil War. He lectured to Irish Americans that:

The Republic, that gave us an asylum and an honorable career—that is the mainstay of human freedom the world over—is threatened with disruption. It is the duty of every liberty-loving citizen to prevent such a calamity at all hazards. Above all, it is the duty of us Irish citizens, who aspired to establish a similar form of government in our native land. It is not only our duty to America, but also to Ireland. We could not hope to succeed in our effort to make Ireland a republic without the moral and material aid of the liberty-loving citizens of these United States. That aid we might rely upon receiving at the proper time. But now, when all the thoughts, energies, and resources of this noble people are needed to preserve their own institutions from destruction—they cannot spare either sympathy, arms or men, for any other cause.

The leader of the Fenian Brotherhood, James Stephens, came to New York just prior to the Civil War in an effort to enlist Meagher in a new struggle for Irish freedom. He failed to do so. It was clear by then that Meagher had broken with his past, and that his future lay in the New World. He seems to have determined that the millions of Irish-Americans had nothing to go back to, and that he must now lead their fight for acceptance in America.

Currier and Ives recognized Meagher's contributions and fame and celebrated them in prints. The state and city of New York have been indifferent to his memory, but a statue erected in Helena, the capital of Montana, honors him.

Print courtesy The Library of Congress

Opposite:
THOMAS FRANCIS MEAGHER

TRIAL OF THE IRISH PATRIOTS AT CLONMEL, OCTOBER 22, 1848

Thomas F. Meagher, Terence B. McManus, and Patrick O'Donohue, are shown receiving their sentences.

The jury was composed of the landed gentry, the rich Protestant landlords and magistrates who were descendants of Cromwell's army and had settled in Tipperary. For the crime of advocating freedom for Ireland Chief Justice Doherty sentenced his fellow countrymen under English Law to be hanged, drawn, and quartered.

The three men in the dock, Meagher, O'Donohue, and McManus, leaders of their Young Ireland movement had been captured after resistance collapsed at the Widow McCormack's house. Meagher and O'Donohue were taken on the road from Holy Cross; McManus made it to a ship, the M. D. *Chase*, in the Cove of Cork before being discovered.

The defendants made no effort to hide their guilt; they knew that the verdict had been predetermined. It could not be more self-evident that to fight for freedom in Tipperary in 1848 was a crime of high treason under English law. Terence McManus was an organizer whose death many years later in the United States would be more significant in one way than his life; as it inspired a new rebellion. Like McManus, Patrick O'Donohue, though a solicitor, was a man of few words. It was left to Thomas

Francis Meagher, the young orator with the golden voice, to speak for all three: "Judged by the laws of England, I know that this crime entails on me the penalty of death, but the history of Ireland explains this crime and justifies it. Judged by that history, I am no criminal and deserve no punishment. Judged by that history, the treason of which I stand convicted loses all guilt, has been sanctified as a duty and will be ennobled as a sacrifice. With these sentiments, I await the sentence of the Court . . . pronounce then, my Lords, the sentence the law directs, and I shall be prepared to hear it. I trust I shall be prepared to meet its execution, I hope I shall be able, with a light heart, and a clear conscience, to appear before a higher tribunal, where a Judge of infinite goodness as well as of infinite justice will preside and where my Lords, many many judgments of this world will be reversed."

All three men were sentenced to death, but the sentence was commuted to life sentences in Van Diemen's Land. All three escaped to the United States after a number of years in Australia.

COLONEL MICHAEL CORCORAN
AT THE BATTLE OF BULL RUN, JULY 21, 1861

When the Irish arrived in force in New York in the early 1850s they reveled in the American right to bear arms. Many joined civilian militia units such as the Emmets & Montgomery Guards and the Phoenix Brigade, as well as New York's 165th Infantry (69th Regiment). They loved the uniforms, the rifles, and the parades, and a few shrewd revolutionary organizers among them encouraged the trend, hoping that in some future war between the United States and England the Irish militias would be ready to spearhead a U.S.-sponsored invasion of Ireland.

War did break out, but it was not the war that the Irish had hoped for. In any event, when the flag was fired on at Fort Sumter in Charleston Harbor, the Irish, more than any other group, were trained and ready to fight. More than 145,000 men born in Ireland and some thirty-eight different Irish regiments would eventually fight for the Union in the Civil War. The first two regiments to reach the field at Bull Run were Irish. In New York, the first regiment to volunteer for active duty was the 69th, led by Michael Corcoran.

Born in County Sligo, Corcoran was, on his mother's side, a descendant of Patrick Sarsfield. He had once served the queen as a member of the Royal Irish Constabulary, which at that time was an instrument of British occupation, but he resigned and emigrated to America at the age of twenty-two. Somewhere along the line he became a member of a conspiratorial organization called the Fenian Brotherhood, whose object was to incite rebellion in Ireland. With the coming of the Civil War, however, all of Corcoran's energies and leadership went into maintaining the Union, while gaining recognition for the Irish through their efforts in that endeavor.

The summer before the outbreak of the Civil War, a court-martial had been filed against Colonel Corcoran for his refusal to parade the 69th Regiment in honor of Queen Victoria's son, Albert, Prince of Wales, a guest of the city. The audacity of the colonel's action brought widespread condemnation on both sides of the Atlantic. With the coming of the Civil War, however, Corcoran and the 69th Regiment were the first to volunteer for service. They had a trained regiment that was ready, willing, and able to fight for the Union. The court-martial was postponed, and the matter quietly forgotten.

At the outbreak of war, the enlistment periods of many men of New York's 69th Regiment were over, but Colonel Corcoran persuaded virtually all of them to remain and go south to defend Washington. Although his authorization was only for fifteen hundred men, six thousand volunteered to go with him. Among the fifteen hundred who departed was Captain Thomas Francis Meagher, leading a unit of one hundred men.

The 69th left New York on April 23, 1861, to the tunes of Irish pipe bands and cheering crowds. They carried their green banner with its golden harp along with the Stars and Stripes and signs that read "Remember Fontenoy," a reference to the battle of an Irish brigade in the service of France that routed England's elite Coldstream Guards. They were conscious that they were continuing the tradition of Patrick Sarsfield who had led his Irish brigade in France after the siege of Limerick. (See the Currier and Ives print on page 38.) A further motivation for the Irish was the knowledge that England favored the breakup of the United States by tacitly supporting the Confederacy.

The 69th was quartered at Georgetown University for a few weeks of training during the month of May. They were visited there by Abraham Lincoln. Sometime later, they were assigned to Arlington Heights, Virginia, where they were used to construct a fort. The War Department named it Fort Corcoran after their leader. When the Union generals were satisfied that Washington's defenses were secure, they prepared for a march on the Confederate capitol at Richmond. The army headed towards Manassas railroad junction on July 16, expecting a quick victory. The 69th Regiment was part of that approach. The Confederate Army had taken up a position behind a stream called the Bull Run. This stream, like the river in the Battle of the Boyne, was easily forded by troops, but getting cannons up the steep bank on the other side was a different story. The ensuing battle would be the first great engagement of the Civil War.

In the first serious action, a Union force, in a successful flanking movement, crossed the Bull Run and rolled up the Confederates on the other side. The 69th, under the general leadership of Colonel William Tecumseh Sherman, was ordered across. They joined the fight, pushing the Confederates along the Warrenton Turnpike until they reached a hill where the rebel batteries were concentrated. Successive charges on the gun implacements by Union battalions failed. The defenders were covered by dense woods behind their cannons.

Stymied by the high bank of the Bull Run, the Union forces were able to bring up no artillery with them and they were unable to dislodge the batteries of the Confederates. Undaunted, however, the 69th came on. Shouting *"Faugh-A-Ballagh"* (Clear the Way) they charged up the hill, many with their shirts off and some without shoes. As they crested the hill, the man carrying the green flag was cut down by a sharpshooter. Another grabbed the

COLONEL MICHAEL CORCORAN

flag, but he too was cut down, and yet another and another. The rebel artillery covered the open ground in front of them and when the 69th charged across it their ranks were devastated by shot and shell. They regrouped and charged again, losing the green flag to the South, although one of their members, John Keefe, regained it. Regrouping, they attacked a third time, to no avail.

Strong Confederate reinforcements had now outflanked the Union side and the 69th had to fall back. Colonel Corcoran regrouped his men in the classic square formation and they began retiring from the field of battle in good order. On passing through a narrow pathway through the woods, the square disintegrated, mingling two Union regiments fleeing from the South's counterattack. Corcoran ran back and grabbed the colors, and like the minstrel boy of old, he drew his sword and stood against the onrush of the Southern cavalry. Captain McIvor, Lieutenant Connelly, and nine non commissioned officers and privates of the 69th returned and stood with him. They were quickly surrounded by the advancing Confederates, who took them prisoner.

In the course of the retreat Thomas Francis Meagher's horse was shot out from under him by a cannon, and he lay senseless on the field. A private from another Federal unit recognized the famous orator on the ground where he lay unconscious and brought him to safety.

Even in defeat the 69th was perhaps the only Union regiment whose reputation survived the Battle of Bull Run. The Southern press paid respect to their courage, though the South had long hoped to dissuade the Irish from joining the abolitionist cause. Indeed, some 40,000 Irish-born immigrants, including John Mitchel's three sons, would eventually take up arms for the Confederacy.

President Lincoln praised the efforts of the 69th. But, as their enlistment period was again up, they were ordered back to New York. Led by Meagher (Corcoran being a prisoner), they marched up Broadway on July 27, 1861, to a glorious welcome from Irish-American societies and the citizens of New York. The *New York Illustrated News* of August 5, 1861, paid tribute: "Let the truth be told. Our men fought bravely and suffered severely before they turned their backs on those accursed batteries; and nobly they purchased, with drops of bloody sweat, the welcome that warm hearts, fair hands and beaming eyes gave them on their return to New York. The 69th left New York 1,500 strong. They returned with about 1,000. The loss is heart-stirring. All honor to the brave!" The write-up, accompanied by a front-page engraving, showed the 69th, stripped to the waist, charging the enemy with their bayonets.

The Irish, as they had done before and would do again, had pulled victory out of defeat. The march up Broadway was, more than anything else, the opening salvo in the fight for acceptance in their adopted country. It was also a blow against the Know-Nothing Party of the day. Colonel Corcoran was in a Confederate prison and the 69th was out of service, but Thomas Francis Meagher, who could now clearly see the road ahead, would use the old 69th as his base.

Currier and Ives made two prints of the 69th's celebrated engagement. Similar in composition, they have different titles. Both prints show the Irish dressed in red and blue, with headgear reminiscent of the French Foreign Legion flowing in the breeze. Not a case of artistic license,

this was correct: before blue and gray became standard, the uniforms of early units on both sides were colorful. Here, too, the pictures show correctly that because of the heat, the 69th had stripped to the waist before advancing.

Currier and Ives apparently adapted both prints from an illustration in *Harper's Weekly* for August 10, 1861. The magazine described the battle, praising the 69th, but made no recognition that it was an Irish regiment. Their account quotes an officer who had been on the scene: "The 69th Regiment, New York State Militia, performed prodigies of valor. They stripped themselves, and dashed into the enemy with the utmost fury. The difficulty was to keep them quiet. While the Second was engaging a regiment of rebels, they retreated into a thick hayfield to draw the Northerners into a trap. The Second continued firing into them, while the 69th, by a flank movement, took them in the rear, and pouring a deadly fire into their ranks, afterward charged them with the bayonet. The slaughter was terrible and the defeat complete, for not a man stirred of the whole 500–600. In this attack, there was very few of the 69th wounded."

BRIGADIER GENERAL MICHAEL CORCORAN

Brigadier General Michael Corcoran at the Head of His Gallant Irish Brigade

The minstrel boy to the war is gone,
in the ranks of death you'll find him.
His father's sword he has girded on,
and his wild harp slung behind him.
"Land of Song!" said the warrior-bard,
"Tho all the world betray thee,
one sword, at least, thy rights shall guard,
one faithful harp shall praise thee!"

Thomas Moore

After his capture at Bull Run, Michael Corcoran remained a Confederate prisoner for approximately a year. His Southern captors tried to induce him to defect. They failed to sway him, however, and though his conduct was regularly criticized by the Richmond press they ultimately declared that "the constant obstinacy of the most impudent and inveterate of the Yankee prisoners, Colonel Corcoran, was preferable, by far, to the repentant profession and cringing course of some prisoners to obtain a parole."

Corcoran received his freedom in an exchange of prisoners and returned to New York on August 22, 1862, to a tumultuous welcome by Mayor Opdyke and large contingents of soldiers, policemen, firemen, and ordinary citizens. Thereafter, he organized the Corcoran Legion, and returned to battle as a brigadier general. He was accidentally killed at the age of thirty-six on December 23, 1863, when he was thrown from his horse at Sawyer's Station, Virginia, after returning from a meeting with Thomas Francis Meagher.

Corcoran was an example of the best the Union Army had to offer in the way of courage and determination. His exploits could not be ignored even by the anti-Irish media of the day. *Harper's Weekly* of August 30, 1862, carried a front-page engraving of the general with a biographical sketch that took note of Corcoran's earlier snubbing of the Prince of Wales. It went on to comment: "It will suffice to say that for that offense, no one will be disposed to censure him now. If Prince Albert Edward were to come here tomorrow, there is not a Colonel in the service who would willingly pay honor to the heir to the throne of a country which has treated us as England has done during the past year."

In the Currier and Ives print, Corcoran is shown as a dashing figure on horseback, waving his sword as he leads his band of determined men to face the enemy. The 69th's battle flag—a harp on a green background—waves behind him. Corcoran is still remembered by his regiment each year as they lead the Saint Patrick's Day Parade up Fifth Avenue to the tune of the "Minstrel Boy."

General Meagher at the Battle of Fair Oaks, Va., June 1, 1862

In foreign fields from Dunkirk to Belgrade,
lie the soldiers and chiefs of the Irish Brigade.

Thomas Davis, circa 1843

In early 1989, while searching for artifacts at the Antietam Battlefield, Civil War buffs found the skeletons of four soldiers at a place called the Sunken Road. The men had been shot dead, and their bodies covered over by natural forces where they had fallen more than a century before.

Scientific examination of the skeletons, one of a man about forty years old with a rosary still around his neck and another wearing a miraculous medal, proved that all four were members of the Irish Brigade, then under the command of Thomas Francis Meagher. They had given as good as they got, as they experienced, with other soldiers of the North and South, one of the bloodiest days in American history. The names of the four are unknown, but the eldest one may well have been John Cavanagh, the man who had been severely wounded in 1848 at the Widow McCormack's house in Ireland and who gave his life for the Union at the Sunken Road.

Captain Meagher returned to New York with his corps after Bull Run, and the 69th was mustered out of service. In the early days of the Civil War it was the practice for a charismatic individual to apply for a commission to raise his own regiment. Meagher got permission to form a unit to be known as the Irish Brigade. The only stipulation was that a general would be named later. Meagher traveled the eastern seaboard from Boston to Philadelphia in search of volunteers. He addressed tens of thousands of people at rallies and celebrations, including a crowd of fifty thousand in New York at a picnic for the widows of the 69th Regiment. At the same time, he preached the demise of the Know-Nothing Party, proclaiming that it was dead, and that the Irish in good conscience could and should join the cause of preserving the Union. Five hundred men from the old 69th rejoined and were combined with the 88th and 63rd New York Volunteers to bring the number up to an authorized limit of 1,500 men. For a while a "Blue Blood" unit, the 29th Massachusetts, was attached to the brigade, but this was replaced by an Irish unit, the 28th Massachusetts, before the Battle of Fredericksburg.

Meagher by this time had his share of opponents, and the consensus was that the leadership of the brigade should be offered to James Shields, a member of the United States Senate and the most venerable Irishman on the scene. Shields had come to America from County Tyrone and was a hero of the Mexican War at the Battles of Cerro Gordo and Chapultepec. He was a popular man, who was elected to the United States Senate three times represent-

GENERAL MEAGHER AT THE BATTLE OF FAIR OAKS

ing three different states. It is likely that he would have been elected president except that the Constitution forbade it by virtue of his foreign birth. Shields was also an activist, who tried to get Irish immigrants to settle on western lands. Illinois towns such as Shieldsville, Erin, and Kilkenny give testimony to his success in this effort. He was on a similar mission in Durango, Mexico, when he was offered the leadership of the Irish Brigade.

On arriving in New York to accept the position, Shields learned that Meagher had already been nominated for the command. He backed Meagher's right to command the brigade, realizing that it was he who had organized it. Shields thereafter got a commission as a general in the regular army and commanded a division at the Battle of Kernstown in the Shenandoah Valley, where he defeated Stonewall Jackson. He was the only Northern general to defeat Jackson in battle. (Wounded later, Jackson died from pneumonia before the end of the war.)

Taking command of the Irish Brigade as a brigadier general, Meagher tried to persuade Congress to bring together the various Irish regiments throughout the army. He asked that a division of approximately fifteen thou-

sand men be formed under the leadership of Shields. Congress, perhaps afraid that the Irish might take too much credit for winning the war, refused this request.

When the North resumed the offensive, the Irish Brigade was attached to the Army of the Potomac. It advanced to Fair Oaks, a suburb of Richmond, under the command of General George McClellan. The Confederates attacked McClellan at Fair Oaks but failed to dislodge the Union army, losing eight thousand men to five thousand on the Union side. The Irish Brigade distinguished itelf by making several charges against various elements of the rebel army. Now recognized by their Gaelic battle cry, *Faugh-A-Ballagh* (Clear the Way), they earned the respect of their commanders and comrades. This was a group to be relied upon in battle and handy to have on the flank in the event of a surprise attack.

The Currier and Ives print gives the impression that the men of the Irish Brigade have broken the Confederate lines and are about to take Richmond on their own. This was not the case, however, and although their casualties were light at Fair Oaks, they lost more than five hundred at Antietam. Worse was yet to come.

In December of 1862, the brigade experienced its most difficult trial in the assault on Fredericksburg under the command of General Burnside, who had replaced McClellan. The brigade entered Fredericksburg and, with other units of the Army on the Potomac, fought a house-to-house battle, pushing the Confederates out of the town to a series of cliffs known as Marye's Heights. The Southern forces on the Heights were commanded by Colonel Robert McMillan and included thousands of Irishmen of the 24th Georgia Brigade.

Against the advice of his subordinates, Burnside ordered a frontal attack on the Heights. Next morning the men of the Irish Brigade, waiting their turn at the bottom of the Heights, saw what was in store for them, as thousands of Union soldiers in front of them were systematically mowed down. It must have been with heavy hearts that Confederate Irishmen on the Heights saw their countrymen, green banners flying, begin to charge up the hill. But with pin point accuracy the defenders mowed down the soldiers of the Irish Brigade. The attackers got to within twenty-five yards of the top before being driven back.

Meagher gathered up what was left of his troops and took them off the field. Of the fifteen hundred men he had led up Marye's Heights only 263 were mustered for parade the next day. When General Hancock asked about the rest of the company, Meagher replied, "General, this is our company."

Thomas Francis Meagher was forced to resign from the Irish Brigade after the Battle of Fredericksburg because of restrictions in recruiting, but his men went on to distinguish themselves at Gettysburg. Just before that engagement, the brigade chaplain, Father Corby (who would later become president of Notre Dame University),

preached in the shadow of Little Round Top to a body now reduced to five hundred men and under the command of Colonel Kelly. Father Corby told the men that to fight and die for the Union guaranteed an eternal reward in heaven. After Mass they went out to battle once more.

The Irish Brigade did their share to keep the Confederates at bay at Gettysburg in those areas of the battlefield known as Little Round Top, the Peach Orchard, Wheat Field, the Devil's Den, and the Valley of Death. They played a significant part in preserving General Meade's left flank, thus forcing General Robert E. Lee to order the now famous Pickett's Charge against Meade's front lines the next day. Sitting on Little Round Top, the brigade were spectators to that event, but the veterans of Fredericksburg must have sympathized with Pickett's men being slaughtered left and right as they advanced on Cemetery Ridge. The thrill of victory for the Union, however, brought cheering through their ranks, in what proved to be the turning point of the war.

If you travel to Gettysburg National Military Park, at a small clearing on Sickles Avenue near the Peach Orchard, you will find a huge bronze Celtic cross on which is depicted an Irish wolfhound. It commemorates the devotion and sacrifice of Irishmen to the Union. A request to erect a similar monument to the Irish Brigade, along with the hundreds of other monuments already in place at the Sunken Road at Antietam Battlefield, has been approved under pressure from the Irish-American community after initial rejection by the National Parks and Monuments Service. And on September 17, 1989, to the tune of the "Minstrel Boy," the four unknown Irish Brigade members were finally buried with full military honors in Arlington National Cemetery.

COL. JAMES A. MULLIGAN OF THE ILLINOIS IRISH BRIGADE

Unlike Michael Corcoran or Thomas Francis Meagher, James A. Mulligan was a native-born Irish-American, coming to life in Utica, New York, in 1829 of immigrant parents. After his father died, when he was very young, his mother moved to Chicago, where she remarried. He was educated at the Catholic College of North Chicago, later studied law, and was admitted to the bar at the age of 27. He was also a second lieutenant in the Chicago Shield Guards and when the Civil War broke out, he organized a meeting of Irish-American companies in the Chicago area. With the endorsement of Senator Douglas of Illinois, he went to Washington and offered to President Lincoln a regiment, which became known as the Illinois Irish Brigade (the 23rd Illinois Regiment).

In September 1861, a few months after the Battle of Bull Run, Mulligan, by then a colonel, and his Illinois Irish Brigade fought the Confederates at Lexington, Missouri. The Union forces in the area were commanded by General John Frémont, who had arranged to store large sums of money belonging to the people of Warrensburg at Lexington, the capital of Lafayette County on the south bank of the Missouri River. The vaults at Lexington also held $800,000 in gold, which the Missouri legislature had abandoned when the city was occupied by Union soldiers. At Lexington, however, the Union forces consisted primarily of home guards, portions of the 8th and 13th Missouri Regiments, and the 1st Illinois Cavalry. Finding himself the senior officer present, Mulligan assumed command of the Union forces, which numbered 2,640 men.

From Jefferson City, 120 miles to the east, General Sterling Price, with twenty-four thousand Confederate soldiers, launched a massive counterattack against Lexington. Ironically from an Irish-Catholic point of view, Colonel Mulligan found himself making a desperate stand at a place called Masonic Hill. The battle raged for eight days, from 12–20 September, with Mulligan holding his ground against all comers. A residence on the perimeter of his position, which was being used as a hospital, was captured by the Confederates, and its surgeon and chaplain were taken prisoner. As things began to look bleak, Mulligan sent Lieutenant Rains and ten men of the Irish Brigade downriver to Jefferson City to bring back reinforcements. But forty miles south of Lexington, Confederates under General Park intercepted their steamer, *Sunshine*, and captured them.

At Masonic Hill, the home guard raised the white flag, but Mulligan hauled it down, refusing General Price's demand of unconditional surrender. The fighting continued, more deadly than before. After all hope was lost, Colonel Mulligan finally gave up the struggle. The Union casualties were three to five hundred killed and wounded; the Confederates lost between two and three thousand men. For his defense of Masonic Hill, Mulligan received the thanks of the United States Congress and the commission of brigadier general. He refused the promotion, preferring to remain Colonel of the 23rd Illinois, which was given the right to use the name Lexington on its colors.

In November 1863 the Union warship *Kearsarge*, under the command of Captain John S. Winslow, while trailing the Confederate raider *Florida* in the North Atlantic, docked at Queenstown, Ireland, for a few days. Word spread that men could sign up on board to join the Union navy, collect a bounty of four hundred dollars, and get free passage to the New World. It was an offer that few Irishmen for miles around could refuse, and the ship was swamped with recruits. Local British authorities got word of the recruiting and stopped it. This activity involving the *Kearsarge* caused considerable friction between England and the United States.

Britain had passed a law called the Foreign Enlistment Act, which made it a crime for its citizens to enlist on either side in the American Civil War, but the act was aimed at the Union, and not enforced against the Confederacy. At the time, in fact, two Confederate raiders, the *Florida* and *Alabama*, built under contract in England and manned by local recruits, were roaming the Atlantic, seizing commercial ships sympathetic to the Union.

In the United States, to appease Britain and keep her at least publicly neutral, federal authorities ordered a court-martial of Captain Winslow, but allowed him to retain his command. By the time he returned to the United States, he had sunk the *Alabama* and was a national hero. There was no one to press charges and the matter was forgotten.

This incident was viewed by the British almost as seriously as the so-called *Trent* Affair of October 1861, when England came to the brink of a war against the United States. In that incident, Captain Charles Wilkes, in command of the *San Jacinto* for the Union, boarded the English steamer *Trent* off the Virgin Islands. He captured James J. Mason and John Slidell, two former U.S. senators who had gone over to the Confederacy and were now Commissioners to England and France. Secretary of State Seward diffused the situation by releasing the two men in order to keep England out of the war.

The incident of the *Kearsarge*, however, was a trauma for the British. The ruling classes favored the war between the states, feeling that it would keep Britain number one. They had smugly sat back with arms folded during the famine in Ireland. Now, however, an unforeseen side effect of the famine was the creation of a large Irish population outside their jurisdiction. That population was actively working against British interests. Emigration from Ireland, which had abated during the early years of the war, rose dramatically in 1863 and 1864 as inducements by the Union to join its forces escalated. The Irishmen who turned up aboard the *Kearsarge* to sign up for the Union navy overnight became "Disloyal British Subjects."

The Currier and Ives print captures this interesting bit of Irish-American history. In it John Bull, holding the Foreign Enlistment Act under his arm, threatens that if Pat fights for the Union he will be treated as a pirate if he is caught. (In fact the English tried and convicted some of the men who had attempted to enlist with Captain Winslow.) Pat, of course, is able to tell John Bull to take his threats and stuff them. The Stars and Stripes he is now fighting for as a member of the Union navy will protect him even from his old enemy, John Bull himself. This is the dialogue under the title:

John Bull: Now Pat. Mind! If you enlist with either of the Belligerents I shan't protect you if you are taken as a pirate.

Pat: (exultingly) Be me soul thin, I don't want your protecshun, the ould stars and stripes there that I'm fightin' for will protect me.

Print courtesy The Library of Congress

James Stephens
Head Center of the Irish Republican Brotherhood

A tombstone in Ireland bears this inscription:

Here lies
James Stephens
Born at Kilkenny
A.D. 1824
died from the effects of a wound
at Ballingarry, 1848
Aged 24 Years
R.I.P.

The coffin buried in this grave, however, contains only stones: James Stephens escaped to France after the attack on the Widow McCormack's house in 1848. Virtually no one, including members of his own family, was aware of the deception. In Paris, Stephens learned the fundamentals of conspiracy and intrigue from radical secret societies that flourished there at that time.

While he was in exile a group of Irish-Americans under the leadership of Colonel John O'Mahoney established an organization called the Fenians in America. The Fenians asked James Stephens to return to Ireland and organize a branch of the group to overthrow British rule and win national independence by force of arms. (The Fenian organization in Ireland was known as the Irish Republican Brotherhood.)

Stephens by this time was a careful, shrewd, and patient conspirator. He was excited by the challenge and agreed to try to organize a new revolt. When he returned home from Paris, he found his father and sister dead and a country depressed from the lingering effects of the famine and the failure of the rebellion of 1848. Ireland at this time was tightly controlled by the British army, but the police and large portions of the army were composed of Irishmen, and these were assiduously cultivated by Stephens and his fellow conspirators. He believed, however, that for a rebellion to succeed it would be necessary to have arms, money, and men from the United States. He believed that men such as John Mitchel, Thomas Francis Meagher, and Colonel John O'Mahoney would be the ones to galvanize this support for him.

Stephens came to America in 1858 to accomplish this task but was disconcerted by what he found. He felt that the Irish exiles had lost their ideals in their pursuit of the almighty dollar. He called the United States "the land of Self, Greed, and Grab." He talked with Meagher, now a prosperous attorney with a house on Fifth Avenue in New York. Meagher wished him well in his endeavors but refused to join him. A pilgrimage to John Mitchel at

Knoxville, Tennessee, was likewise fruitless. Mitchel felt that an insurrection was pointless as long as England had no active enemies in the world. To him, an English war with either the United States or France was a minimum prerequisite for any attempt to free Ireland. Colonel O'Mahoney came through for Stephens, but did not have the influence that Meagher or Mitchel could muster. Overall, the support he received was meager.

In 1861 lightning struck for Stephens and the Fenian movement at home and in America with the death in San Francisco of Terence McManus. (McManus is one of the three men shown in the Currier and Ives print *The Trial of the Irish Patriots at Clonmel*.) McManus's body was transported by train across America on its way home to Ireland. Demonstrations for Irish freedom at various points caught the media's attention, and a sermon by Archishop Hughes at Old Saint Patrick's Cathedral gave the demonstrators the legitimacy they sought.

From New York, McManus's body was sent to the Cove of Cork where 100,000 people turned out to pay respects. It was then sent on to Dublin, where many more came out for a torchlight parade. The Fenian movement had reached its zenith and James Stephens as its Head Center was the man of the hour. But peaceful demonstrations, even those involving the whole country, would not sway the English.

The movement waned while Stephens waited for arms to arrive from America to begin the rebellion. In 1864, Stephens was captured by the English, and earned international headlines with a daring escape a few days later. He accomplished this with the help of his jailers, proving his boast that he had agents everywhere in Ireland. Nevertheless, there would be no rebellion, at least for Stephens. In December 1866, at a meeting in New York, impatient fellow leaders removed him as Head Center and replaced him. Since the Fenians had been organized by the exiles, Stephens depended on them for support. Having lost it, he made his way forlornly to France again as the movement in Ireland was crippled by searches, raids, and arrests.

The rebellion, of course, did happen in 1867 and its outcome was inevitable. The rising was a disaster, a fiasco exceeded only by that of 1848. The fighting men were smothered by snow, sleet, and rain and then crushed by the army and constabulary. Yet, as thousands of Fenians marched virtually unarmed to fight for Ireland's freedom, and littered the open roads with their dead bodies, they left behind an indelible mark on their nation's conscience. The men of '67 would never be forgotten.

Stephens watched from France as another parade of revolutionaries were sentenced to long terms of penal servitude. The leaders, Colonel Kelly and Captain Deasy, were freed in a daring raid in Manchester, England. They were never recaptured, but their rescuers, Allen, Larkin, and O'Brien, were caught and hanged, crying, "God save Ireland." They are remembered in song and verse to this day.

Stephens, a Catholic, spent twenty-five years in exile in Paris. At the end of that time an Irish Protestant landlord intervened on his behalf with the British government and the old Fenian was allowed to return home, where he lived with his wife until his death in 1901. The landlord's name was Charles Stewart Parnell.

Note: this print is not by Currier and Ives, but by a contemporary.
Print courtesy The Library of Congress

COL. JOHN O'MAHONEY:
HEAD CENTER OF THE FENIAN BROTHERHOOD

John O'Mahoney founded the Fenian movement in New York in 1858. He copied the name Fenian from *Na Fianna,* Gaelic for a group of men, such as we have seen were led by the ancient Celtic warrior Finn MacCool in the province of Munster. O'Mahoney, from County Cork, had organized his own *fianna* of two thousand men in County Tipperary during the 1848 uprising, but they failed to see any action. O'Mahoney fled to Paris with James Stephens, but later came to America. When the Civil War began, he organized a regiment of Fenians, which became known as the 99th New York National Guard. He was appointed honorary colonel for this effort.

Soon after its foundation, however, the New York Fenian organization developed internal divisions. Two factions emerged, those who wished to concentrate the energies of the movement in support of a rebellion in Ireland, and others who felt that the best course of action was to attack Canada. Those who favored the incursion into Canada, which was not yet unified into the provinces that we know today, planned to establish an independent Irish state on this continent by taking over that area of Canada generally known as Acadia (roughly New Brunswick today). They hoped to encourage Irish immigrants to settle there.

A secondary and less defined goal of the Canadian invasion was to attack the forces of the British crown where they were most vulnerable. At the very least, with this threat of force, the Fenians hoped to create better conditions for their countrymen back home in Ireland. There were also some who thought that if they could gain possession of a part of Canada, they could somehow trade it back to the British for the freedom of Ireland. O'Mahoney opposed the Canadian venture, but in doing so lost control of the majority of the organization.

In an attempt to steal the thunder of the Canadian faction, O'Mahoney decided to make his own attack in the north. His target was Campobello Island, off the coast of Maine. At that time, Campobello was neutral territory, claimed by both the United States and Britain. O'Mahoney thought that the United States would not condemn such an attack, though the British might see it as an act of aggression. Perhaps war would follow, giving the planned insurrection in Ireland a chance of success.

In April of 1866 O'Mahoney and a few hundred men congregated along the frontier. Unarmed for the most part, they waited for the arrival of the Fenian steamer *Ocean Spray*, loaded with guns and ammunition. Before it could land, however, U. S. General George Meade arrived on the scene and quickly put an end to the adven-

A photograph of John O'Mahoney by Matthew Brady.
Courtesy the Library of Congress

ture. O'Mahoney lost credibility with this failure and his faction lost out among the Fenians to William S. Roberts.

Now considerably weakened in power, O'Mahoney concentrated on helping James Stephens by sending money and arms to Ireland. But, as we have seen, he lacked organizational ability. For the abortive revolution of 1867 O'Mahoney sent a ship from New York called *Erin's Hope* with thirty-eight Civil War veterans and five thousand guns. The ship arrived in Donegal on May 23, 1867, two full months after the rebellion had ended. All aboard were arrested.

John O'Mahoney's last days were spent in abject poverty in New York. A friend found him dying in a broken-down garret in 1877 and after his death made arrangements to have his body transported back to Ireland. There, a grateful people showed their appreciation for his efforts for Irish freedom by turning out in thousands for his funeral.

A tombstone in Holy Cross Cemetery at Lackawanna in upstate New York reads:

In Memory Of
Edward K. Lonergan
Lieut. 7th Reg't. I.R.A.
Aged 21 Years
Who Fell, Gallantly Fighting
Ireland's Enemies, On
The Famous Field Of
Ridgeway
June 2, 1867
Requiscat In Pace

The headstone tells the story of a young man who gave his life for the Irish Republican Army in 1867 in North America. Not many Americans, or Irish for that matter, are aware that an army of Civil War veterans, numbering approximately eight hundred men under the command of Captain John O'Neill and calling themselves the Irish Republican Army, crossed Lake Erie from the United States to attack Canada in 1867.

O'Neill's invasion was met by a superior force of Canadian and British troops at a place called Ridgeway, but in the pitched battle that followed the Civil War veterans of the Irish Republican Army routed the queen's soldiers. However, other units of the IRA, perhaps twenty thousand in all, along the Canadian border failed to attack in support of O'Neill, allowing the Canadians and British to regroup and repulse the invaders. O'Neill was forced to withdraw to the United States, where he surrendered to General George Meade, who had been sent by the U.S. government to prevent any entanglement with Britain over Canada.

This Irish Republican Army was created by the Fenians, a group that had been organized in 1858, but which was dormant during the Civil War. The end of the war left 100,000 Irish combat veterans still not fully integrated into American society, and still deeply concerned about the situation in the old country. For some of them, the attack on Canada seemed a perfect outlet for their energies. Anti-British feeling in the United States as well as latent American designs on Canada helped to create conditions which the Fenians hoped to exploit. The North had been angered by perceived British support for the Confederacy. The South, disappointed by the failure of Britain to come to its aid actively, ignored the activities of the Fenians in that region. The United States government openly sold them surplus Civil War arms. The Fenians, however, because of divisions among their leaders and the lack of sufficient money and proper organization, were only able to get a few thousand men into Canada. Presi-

dent Andrew Johnson eventually decided that the United States could not tolerate the existence of this private army on its soil and intervened to disband it. As a result, the Irish Republican Army that formed up for the attack on Canada numbered only eight hundred.

Casualties on the battlefield at Ridgeway were relatively light. The Canadians suffered thirteen dead and fifty-seven wounded, and the Fenian casualties were fewer. Meanwhile, in New York City the *New York Herald* stirred the Irish community by claiming that but for the actions of the United States Army in intervening, the Fenians would have overrun Canada. The Canadians, for their part, were appalled by the invasion and that loose confederation of provinces was jolted into voting for a strong federation some time later. It is doubtful that the Canada of today gives any credit to the Irish Republican Army for the positive effect it had on the formation of their country, but since in recent times they have seen fit to elect Brian Mulroney, a son of the shamrock, as prime minister, we can presume that all is forgiven.

The leader of the Canadian raid, Captain John O'Neill, was sentenced to two years in prison at Burlington, Vermont, for his role in the invasion, but was pardoned by President Grant after serving one month because of pressure from the Irish community. Irrepressible, O'Neill led forty Fenians across the Canadian border from Minnesota in October 1871 and attacked the Hudson Bay Company. He was again arrested, but this time was released without a prison sentence. Thereafter, he devoted his energies to establishing Irish-American settlements in the state of Nebraska, where a town is named for him.

The eight-hundred-man assault on Canada involved the single largest force ever put into action by the Irish Republican Army. For the insurrection in Ireland of 1916, Patrick Pearse and James Connolly could only muster six hundred men in Dublin, although that action sparked a guerrilla war that led to the formation of the Irish Free State. The Fenian attack on Canada was, in a way, the first shot fired in the long struggle that culminated in the treaty of 1922, when the IRA won the withdrawal of British forces from four-fifths of Ireland.

(A side story of the Fenians' activity in the United States is their financing of the efforts of John Holland to create a new weapon designed to attack British ships from underwater. This first submarine was called the Fenian Ram, but it never saw action for the IRA. Holland, a former teacher from County Clare, later designed and built the first submarines used by the U. S. Navy. A later Fenian Ram, built in 1881, is on display at the Paterson Museum in Paterson, New Jersey.)

Print courtesy The Library of Congress

Charles Stewart Parnell, M.P.

He was the General Patton of the U.S. Navy in the War of 1812. His name was Charles Stewart and he commanded the American warship *Constitution*. He had no equal in maneuvering a sailing ship and could attack with a dash and a dare that was unparalleled on the high seas. British warships had standing orders not to attack the *Constitution* unless they had a superiority of two to one. In fact, no British ship was allowed to patrol the waters from the Chesapeake to Boston Harbor without an escort, but even that strategy did not save them. Stewart roamed the high seas with an almost psychic flair for finding the enemy. In 1814 off the coast of Madeira he got on the trail of two British fighters, H.M.S. *Cyane* under Captain Gordon Falcon and her consort, the *Levant* under the Hon. George Douglass. The British ships evaded contact until nightfall, and then turned and confidently attacked. With the moon rising across islands of clouds in the sky, Commander Stewart, later affectionately known as "Old Ironsides," first raked the *Cyane* with heavy shot, and before the smoke cleared he had also broadsided the *Levant*, capturing both vessels and hauling them back to the United States with their captains and crews.

This descendant of Ulster Presbyterians would later go on to become first Admiral of the Navy, and if the British thought he was finished with them after the war they were wrong. His daughter, Delia, married the son of the Anglo-Irish aristocrat John Parnell from County Wicklow and the couple gave "Old Ironsides" a grandson to be proud of in his old age, Charles Stewart Parnell.

Charles Stewart Parnell, who as a slender, pale-faced young man had been shy and withdrawn, was destined to have a parliamentary career that would earn him the title of the "uncrowned King of Ireland." He was unlucky in his love for an American heiress but enjoyed the life of a Protestant aristocrat supported by a wealthy father and his American mother in the beautiful mansion called Avondale in the Vale of Avoca, County Wicklow.

Parnell's interest in politics began with the profound drama of the American Civil War, followed by the futile Fenian rising of 1867 in his father's country. The Civil War raised many arguments among his ten brothers and sisters because of their strong ties to the United States. Charles favored the North's fight to rid the country of slavery, but he was also sympathetic to the South's demand for freedom from the federal government.

The political situation in Ireland had changed since the era of Daniel O'Connell due to the liberalization of voting requirements. The majority of the approximately sixty delegates representing Ireland in the British parliament were now Catholic. However, because of the expense of traveling to London and maintaining a residence there it was still not unusual for a wealthy Protestant to represent a Catholic area. Thus, the Protestant landlord Parnell, as an advocate of tenants' rights and, through his mother, a friend of the Fenians, was elected a member of the Irish Parliamentary Party to the House of Commons in England in 1875 from a predominantly Catholic district. Eventually he took up the mantle of O'Connell in the quest for an Irish parliament independent of Britain, though loyal to its queen. This arrangement would have been satisfactory to Parnell but he accepted the likelihood that the Catholic majority would in time move the country to complete independence.

The increasing representation of Irish Catholics in the British parliament still made no change in the lives of the vast Irish peasant class. A decade after the abortive Fenian rising of 1867 conditions had deteriorated. Recurring famine in the years 1879 and 1880, together with insupportable rents charged by absentee landlords, had made life extremely difficult. Widespread evictions of tenants spawned the growth of various secret societies, such as the White Boys and the Invincibles. These groups assassinated landlords and their agents in increasing numbers throughout the country and their acts collectively became known as the "Revenge of Captain Moonlight."

The stage was set for the formation of an organization called the Land League, which was initially led by Michael Davitt. The objective of the Land League was to secure the right of non-eviction and to arrange that the payment of rent should count toward eventual ownership of the land by the tenants. The hope was that in the long term the Catholic Irish could expect that the land would be returned to them. Taking over as leader of the Land League, Parnell devised a new and revolutionary tactic, which became known as "The Land War." At a speech in Ennis on September 19, 1881, he outlined his plan:

> When a man takes a farm from which another has been evicted, you must show him on the roadside when you meet him, you must show him in the streets and the town, you must show him at the shop counter, you must show him in the fair and in the marketplace, and even in the house of worship by leaving him severely alone. By putting him into a moral Coventry, by isolating him from his kind as if he was a leper of old—you must show him your detestation of the crime he has committed.

The first victim of this subtle, new policy was the agent of Lord Erne, Captain Charles Boycott. It worked so well that a new word entered the English language. The power

of the Land League under Parnell expanded throughout the country. Parnell's mother and sister Fanny organized a companion support organization in the United States.

The British government's reaction to Parnell's challenge was typical; habeas corpus was suspended yet again and parliament, now under Gladstone, passed the Coercion Act. Parnell was arrested and sent to Kilmainham Jail as a political prisoner. The League responded with a No Rent Manifesto, and violence related to agrarian reform became more widespread than ever. The government had to deal with Parnell. The result, as his brother reported, was the unwritten Kilmainham Treaty, whereby habeas corpus was restored, the Coercion Act was repealed, and Parnell was freed from prison, with a promise to attempt to influence his followers away from violence. Further, a Compromise Land Act was passed, which guaranteed tenure and fair rent for tenants. Subsequent legislation provided government assistance to enable tenants to purchase their holdings. Although these concessions won by Parnell brought gains, it became clear to a great number of his Fenian supporters that he was a creature of parliament, a crafty politician who, nevertheless, could settle for something short of their dreams.

More than any other Irish leader up to that time, Parnell had wide support in America. He visited the United States and Canada in 1880 to raise funds and drum up political support for the Land League. His brother reported that "the whole of New York after this went mad over the Irish cause, and the Ambassadors of home rule were cordially received by all grades of society." Parnell even addressed the House of Representatives in Washington. He was, however, received warily by the Clan-na-gael, the successor of the Fenian movement: a number of its leaders were distressed by his constitutional approach. This was reflected by hostile demonstrations upon his return to Ireland, especially at Enniscorty in County Wexford. Despite this opposition, however, the Irish at home and abroad were well represented by Parnell. On his shoulders rested the hopes of the Irish people for an independent homeland.

With the abeyance of tenant agitation in 1882, Parnell concentrated on O'Connell's dream of obtaining Home Rule. Shortly after entering parliament, Parnell realized that a few Irish members led by Joseph Biggar had inadvertently stumbled on a new technique. Biggar could not put two sentences together, let alone give a speech, but he could read, and occasionally he read copious extracts from various documents for hours on end, thereby keeping the right honorable English gentleman from doing anything else. Biggar read and read until he exhausted their patience and drove them crazy. He thrived on their contempt.

Most of the Irish delegates considered Biggar to be uncivilized and a disgrace to the Irish nation. Parnell seized on his tactic of obstruction and persuaded the rest of the Irish Party to accept it, thus saying in effect to his English colleagues: if you will legislate nothing of importance to Ireland, we will prevent you from legislating anything of importance to England.

Parnell was now a marked man. The day of the duel was gone, but the day of libel had dawned. After biding their time, Parnell's opposition would use a double murder as a pretext to libel him, attempting to destroy his reputation and leadership.

The situation emerged as follows: on May 6, 1882, Lord Frederick Cavendish arrived in Dublin as the new Chief Secretary of Ireland. On that same day he was walking to his residence through Phoenix Park with his undersecretary, T. H. Burke. Both men were set upon and stabbed to death by assassins from a group called the Invincibles, an extremist offshoot of the Fenians.

England was enraged. Parnell, like all the constitutionalists in Ireland, denounced the act as criminal. Some time later, however, the London *Times* published a series of letters purportedly signed by Parnell suggesting that Cavendish and Burke had got what they deserved. A parliamentary hearing was called to investigate the charges and, under a brilliant cross-examination, a witness called Piggot was shown to be the forger of the letters. Parnell was vindicated. He was returned to parliament more powerful than ever, his party now having grown to eighty-five members.

Under Parnell's leadership, since 1885 the party had held the balance of power between the British Liberal and Tory parties. In 1886 Prime Minister Gladstone made an effort to satisfy the wishes of Parnell's group. He put forward a Home Rule measure that would set up an Irish parliament. That body would have authority to control the local police, but direction of the army and foreign affairs would remain in London. Further, Ireland would no longer have representation in the House of Commons. The measure failed when some of the Liberals voted against their own party.

The movement toward Home Rule could not be stopped, however, and success for a second Home Rule Bill seemed inevitable. Parnell himself said: "It is not now a question of self-government for Ireland; it is only a question as to how much self-government they will be able to cheat us out of."

But like a bombshell, Home Rule was, indeed, stopped. Not by any parliamentary maneuvers but by a beautiful, vivacious woman, Kitty O'Shea. Kitty's husband, Captain O'Shea, filed for divorce in England on the grounds of adultery and named Parnell as co-respondent. Unknown by most, however, was that for ten years the bachelor Parnell had carried on an affair with the beautiful Kitty, having three children with her, and all with the tacit approval of Captain O'Shea. Parnell had even helped O'Shea to get a seat in parliament, where he acted as a go-between to Gladstone in the negotiations for Home Rule.

When the scandal broke Parnell at first had the backing of the Irish Party despite the revelations. They knew of the liaison even though the general public did not. But Gladstone, seeing a chance to remove the powerful Parnell, demanded his resignation from the Irish Party before he would agree to push forward the final Home Rule Bill. The party split. A former ally, T. M. Healy, turned against him. Then, a new and more influential adversary, the hierarchy of the Catholic church, joined the fray, backing Healy's attacks on the moral turpitude of the Protestant leader.

Parnell decided to fight to retain his position, but in election after election his candidates went down to defeat against the combined forces of Healy and the bishops.

Now only forty-five years old, but worn out and in fragile health, he married his Kitty, only to die four months later, in October 1891, of rheumatic fever.

The dream of Home Rule, and with it the last chance for the English to square things with the Irish without violence, died with Parnell. His tragic and romantic figure and ultimate fall from grace left bitter memories and divisions in the Irish psyche. Arguments about the involvement of the church in his downfall and whether he was an adulterer or the "uncrowned king" would be debated throughout the country.

A statue of Parnell in Dublin at the north end of O'Connell Street quotes on its base one of his famous thoughts: "No man has the right to fix the boundary to the march of a nation; no man has the right to say to his country—this far thou shall go and no further."

SCENES IN
THE UNITED STATES

At least thirty-five thousand immigrants made the voyage from Ireland to the United States each year beginning in the early 1840s and continuing past the turn of the century. The fare was relatively low, and with good sailing conditions the trip across the ocean could be made in twenty-one days. Heightening poverty conditions at home made life increasingly difficult, and more and more the Irish turned their backs on Britain and Europe and looked to the United States.

Pre-famine Ireland had an exploding population, which peaked at just over eight million in the year 1841. (By the end of the century, it would be down to four million.) The vast majority of these people were peasants, who leased plots of land from aristocratic, absentee landlords. Most of what they raised or grew went to the landlords in rent payments. With each succeeding generation, the leasehold or plot of land was subdivided between the children, so that the plots became smaller and smaller. There were no great urban industrial centers to attract the poor in Ireland as there were in England and on the Continent, so the great majority of people stayed on the land, and starved. The one great hope that beckoned to them was across the Atlantic in the New World.

The first print of this section is entitled *Outward Bound—New York,* and it is clear that this countryman is going to spend his last copper on the *Shamrock.* As the immigrant tide swelled in 1848 to 200,000 immigrants a year and continued at that level for the next six years, conditions on board the ships deteriorated drastically. Every possible vessel, many of them unseaworthy, was put into service by unscrupulous owners to take advantage of the immigrant tide. Hundreds of men, women, and children were cramped into steerage quarters, where they had little light and air and few sanitary facilities. If the wind was against them, the sailing to the United States could take more than eight weeks.

During this period more than sixty immigrant ships were lost at sea, most by shipwreck, some by fire. These conditions did not abate until the advance of steamers to replace sailing ships in the late 1850s, when the crossing became relatively safe and the journey took less than two weeks.

In the United States the Irish were free from the landlords, but still had to work hard to feed their families. Some were exploited badly by their employers and many could only find jobs in mines, on railroad lines, and in factories with primitive working conditions. There were occasions when they had to stand up as a group to fight for their rights. Something in the Irish character led them sometimes to fight for frivolous causes, but they also stood up for noble ones like the Civil War. Currier and Ives captured one of the Irish protest demonstrations in *The Great Riot at the Astor Place Opera House.*

As the years went by, Irish-Americans acquired the money and leisure to broaden their outlook on life. They could enjoy evenings at the theater or attend sporting events. Some became playwrights and composers. One song and dance team called Harrigan and Hart broke the color barrier and put blacks and Irish together on the stage. An Irish-born author, Dion Boucicault, had many great successes on Broadway, once with a play called *The Shaughraun.* The print of that name shows many facets of Irish life. In the lithograph called *The Man Who Gave Barnum His Turn*, Currier and Ives even suggest that common immigrants could mingle with the rich.

More than anything, however, the hard but welcome work of building roads, canals, and railroads—as well as carrying bricks and mortar for the construction of rows and rows of red brick city apartment houses—ended the deprivation caused by the famine.

Among the children of this new group of citizens were some of the greatest athletes of their time. In the 1880s, the Irish so dominated the new game of baseball that their rivals complained that they were physically superior. This was also evident in boxing, the primary sport of the era, into which Irish-Americans infused a new life and virtually dominated all weight classes for many years. Currier and Ives popularized the champions of the era and helped make them folk heroes to the entire country.

I have chosen to conclude this section with the print *Homeward Bound—New York.* Now, it is a much more prosperous-looking individual studying the sailing schedules from New York to Dublin. This man has the resources to return, but, unlike the peasant in *Outward Bound*, it is not clear that he will, in fact, board the ship to return home. He carries no bags and has no trunks on the dock. His home is now the United States. Ireland is a place of memory. The advertisement for the trip that he is studying may merely evoke nostalgia. It is uncertain whether this reservoir of feeling or mere curiosity will lead him to journey back to the old country.

Print courtesy The Metropolitan Museum of Art, New York

Outward Bound—New York

GREAT RIOT AT THE ASTOR PLACE OPERA HOUSE, NEW YORK

It was a time when acting was in vogue and English actors were the best and most famous of all. Britannia ruled the stage. But it also was a time when the winds of change were blowing in the wings, and the Americans had gathered a small armada of actors of their own who were challenging Britannia's rule.

One such challenger was an American named Edwin Forrest from Philadelphia, who had gained some fame as a Shakespearean and who was touted by the local critics to be the equal of any English actor of the day. Forrest had already done his best to assault the reputation of William Charles Macready, who considered himself the best of all Shakespearean actors of his time. A number of years before, in a provocation akin to the Boston Tea Party, Forrest had booed a Macready performance of *Hamlet* during his own tour of England in 1845.

Macready's opportunity to even the score and suppress the rebellion came in 1849, when Forrest was giving a performance as Macbeth at the Broadway Theatre in New York City. Macready happened to be in town and with the help of some local Tories and other admirers of

John Bull he staged his own *Macbeth* at the Astor Place Opera House.

The Tories and the other British supporters, however, did not reckon with the Irish, a new element on the American scene. Especially concentrated in New York, the Irish were not about to let some English actor get away with this insult to one of their local lads, even if the lad was not Irish himself.

As the print shows, a huge crowd of Irish-Americans surrounded the opera house. A few managed to get inside, where Macready was lucky to escape the fate of Macbeth's victim, Duncan. So great was the stir that the military were called in to protect the audience, as well as Macready. In the end, twenty-two people were dead, and many others wounded. Macready was run out of town.

The riot did little damage to the reputations of Irish-American in New York, however, since they were seen as upholding the honor of a local American actor against the insult of a foreigner.

Print courtesy The Library of Congress

The Man Who Gave Barnum His "Turn"

This story is taken from a real-life incident and is related entirely in the print. The scene is Tom Higgins's barbershop. Enter Phineas T. Barnum:

"Tom, I am in a hurry."
"Sorry for it, Mr. Barnum, but it's that gentleman's turn next."
Barnum to gentleman from Ireland:
"My friend, if you let me have your turn, I'll pay for what you have done."
Gentleman consents, and the following is what the gentleman had done:
    Bath . . . . .25 cents
    Shaving . . . . .10 cents
    Shampooing . . . . .25 cents
    Hair Cutting . . . . .25 cents
    Hair Dyeing . . . . .50 cents
    Hair Curling . . . . .25 cents
    TOTAL COST OF TURN $1.60

The Irishman, in effect, took everything that the shop had to offer and the print shows the transformation in his appearance.

The real story of the print, however, is that Nathaniel Currier and P. T. Barnum were both noteworthy people of New York City. They were good friends and undoubtedly shared the same barber, Mr. Higgins. On hearing of the incident from Mr. Higgins, Currier seized the opportunity to poke fun at his good friend and ran off hundreds of the prints, selling them all over town.

I wonder if Barnum took the print in the spirit in which it was intended, or did he react with outrage as he may have done when presented with the bill for $1.60?

The Irishman's reaction to the print is not recorded, but he was probably not too happy with the artist either.

THE GREAT WALK. "GO AS YOU PLEASE".
THE START.

THE GREAT WALK. "COME IN AS YOU CAN".
THE FINISH.

The sport started when Ed Weston lost a bet that Abe Lincoln would never be president. As a result, he had to walk the 478 miles from Boston to Washington in 1861 to attend Abe's inauguration. His achievement caught the imagination of a people depressed by the impending prospect of a civil war. The sport of long-distance walking was born. For the spectators in those days it was as exciting as the Indianapolis 500 and they cheered as their favorite contestants rounded the turn in an indoor rink as many as two thousand times. In some respects it was like the marathon dancing of the depression era, a physical endurance contest to rival all others.

On March 29, 1879, *Harper's Weekly* reported that "no sporting event has caused so much excitement in New York for many years as the Great Walking Match at Gilmore's Garden between four redoubtable contestants," one of whom held the belt as the "champion of the world." It was referring to America's O'Leary, who competed with Charles Rowell from England and John Ennis from Ireland. It was a five-day event, played to a packed house, with hundreds more people trying to get tickets outside. After about 450 miles, Rowell decided to liven things up and began jogging around the track to the tune of "Yankee Doodle." Ennis, from County Longford, kept the new pace while biding his time in the second position. The defending champion, O'Leary, who had won the title in England but like many sports heroes had been lured by the easy life, was now out of shape for the match and did not even make it halfway before being "locked up for repairs." With the champion gone, Ennis was now the sentimental favorite of the American crowd with its large contingent of Irish. It was to be England's day, however, as Rowell won decisively, covering five hundred miles and 180 yards in five days, nineteen hours, fifty-eight minutes and five seconds. As shown in a sketch from Frank Leslie's illustrated newspaper of March 29, 1879, Ennis was a good sportsman who congratulated Rowell on his victory and rebuked the crowd for their disorderly behavior.

Rowell would later go on to establish a record of 556 miles in six days, an accomplishment that has never been equaled. Ed Weston, who started it all but who preferred to stay outdoors, walked from New York City to San Francisco in 104 days when he was seventy years old.

JOHN ENNIS—THE CELEBRATED PEDESTRIAN

Opposite above:
THE GREAT WALK—GO AS YOU PLEASE

Opposite below:
THE GREAT WALK—COME IN AS YOU CAN

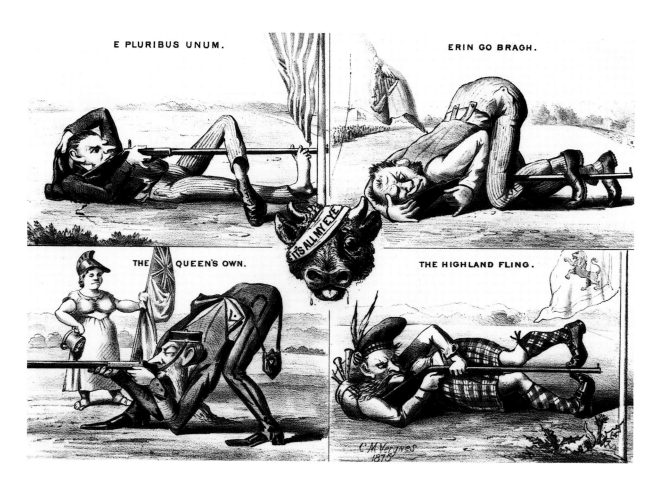

E PLURIBUS UNUM.

ERIN GO BRAGH.

THE QUEEN'S OWN.

THE HIGHLAND FLING.

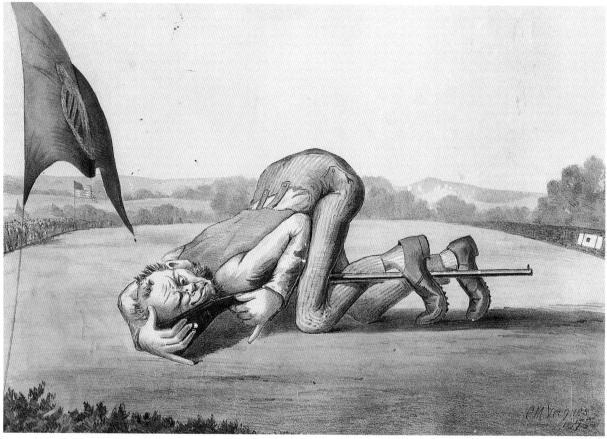

Ye boys of the sod, to Columbia true,
Come up boys and fight for Red, White, and Blue!
Two countries we love and two mottoes we'll share,
And we'll join them in one on the banner we bear:
Erin, mavourneen! Columbia, agra!
E Pluribus Unum! Erin, go bragh!

Song of the Irish Legion by James De Mille,
American Civil War, 1861

In 1910 W. W. Greener, a British arms manufacturer and author, wrote "Long range rifle shooting is the most difficult, requiring finer training, wide knowledge, steadier nerve, and better physique than is demanded of the follower of any other sport."

The sport originated in medieval times in Switzerland with the development of firearms. By the eighteenth century the Swiss were the finest marksmen in the world. In the 1870s the British took up the sport, and they were soon challenged by the Americans. The British relied on muzzleloading rifles, while Americans favored their newly developed breechloaders.

In 1874 an Irish team using muzzleloaders came to Creedmore, Long Island for round one of the "Great International Rifle Match," and put American arms and skill to the test. The Irish marksmen lost to the U.S.A. by a mere three points. A local newspaper artist captured the contorted positions of the shooters and Currier and Ives appropriated that image, modifying it to poke fun at the participants in *The Crack Shots.* Despite the mocking attitude in this print, Currier and Ives were quick to picture the new sport, which attracted substantial crowds.

In later round-robin matches at Dollymount in Ireland and Wimbledon in England, American skill demonstrated beyond question the superiority of the breechloading rifle. To Britain's embarrassment, their team never had any luck and at Creedmore in 1876 only Ireland, Scotland, Australia, and Canada sent competing teams. Again the Irish were narrowly beaten by the U.S. team, with J.K. Milner of Ireland making a record high score of fifteen consecutive bullseyes at one thousand yards. Britain remained embarrassed even after developing a capable breechloading rifle, which was used by the Irish to defeat the Americans at Dollymount in 1880.

In the war to suppress the Boers of South Africa, often thought of as the first modern war, Britain's early failures in the field were deemed the result of the inability of its fighting men to shoot straight. Mr. Greener would lament "The woeful ignorance of many of our hastily gathered levies of even the rudiments of rifle shooting, and consequent failure in the field, quickly brought home to the public mind, the absolute need for some preliminary training in this 'art.'"

The Crack Shots in Position courtesy The Library of Congress

Opposite above:
THE CRACK SHOTS, IN POSITION

Opposite below:
ERIN GO BRAGH!

ACT II, SCENE I, THE SHAUGHRAUN

Dion Boucicault's play *The Shaughraun,* was a sensation. It played to packed houses at Wallach's Theater on Broadway at Thirteenth Street from its opening on November l4, l874 until it closed, producing more money for its backers than any play up to that time. The proceeds for the first Thanksgiving matinee alone was the then unbelievable sum of $2,550.50.

The driving force behind the play was Boucicault himself, born in Dublin and the drama's star, author, and director. A mercurial personality , Boucicault was playing his alter ego, Conn O'Kelly, better known as Conn the Shaughraun. Loosely translated from the Gaelic, Shaughraun means vagabond or ne'er-do-well. An excerpt from the play in which Conn's mother is talking to his sister shows how Boucicault illuminated the Shaughraun's character:

Mrs. O'Kelly: Conn niver did an honest day's work in
    his life. But dhrinkin', an' fishin', an' shooting',
    an' sportin', an' love makin."
Moya: "Sure, that's how the quality pass their lives."
Mrs. O'Kelly: "That's it. A poor man that spoorts the
    sowl of a gentleman is called a blackguard".

Boucicault's rendition of the character of the Shaughraun, accompanied by his faithful dog, Tatters, accounted for the show's dramatic success. The plot itself was secondary. The story is set in Ireland after the Fenian Insurrection of 1867 when a man, tried and sentenced to exile in Australia, escapes to America. He returns for a visit to the old country and is rearrested, after being denounced by an informer, but is restored to freedom by a general pardon.

Boucicault later took the show to London for a repeat of its Broadway success. After 200,000 Londoners had seen the play and cheered loudest at the announcement of the general pardon, the playwright wrote to Prime Minister Disraeli pleading for leniency, and requesting a pardon for the real-life Fenian prisoners then in jail. The request was acknowledged neither by Disraeli nor by any arm of the government.

The scene depicted in the Currier and Ives print is not quite consistent with the action in the play, but without a doubt it captures the mood and character of the Shaughraun. Currier and Ives made a companion print entitled *Snap Apple Night.* In it the same scene is enlarged to include a picture of Saint Patrick looking down on a wild celebration of Halloween, start of the Celtic New Year and the winter festival of the old druid religion.

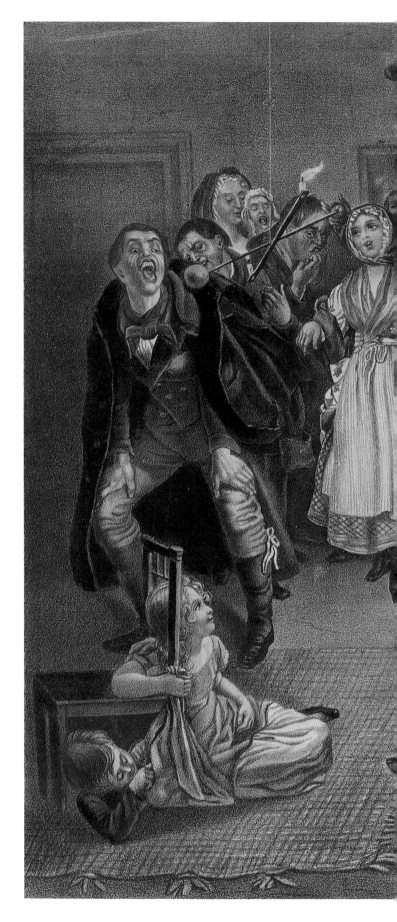

THE GREAT FIGHT FOR THE CHAMPIONSHIP

Championship boxing in America was just getting organized in the 1840s as large-scale Irish immigration was underway. Some of the Irish quickly saw this sport as a path to success in the New World. One of these men, 155 pounds of sinew and muscle, exploded like a game cock in the prize ring and became, pound for pound, the greatest fighter of his time. They called him Yankee Sullivan, but his real name was James Ambrose and he was born in Banden, County Cork.

Like many Irishmen of his time Sullivan had been sentenced by the British to exile in the Australian penal colony of Botany Bay. It is likely that he was an ordinary criminal rather than a revolutionary. Like the patriots Mitchel and Meagher he escaped to America. Now he was again fighting for his life, as he had done many times before, but on this occasion his struggle caught the attention of the entire sporting world of the United States.

The place was called Poole's Island, a scrap of land in Chesapeake Bay of disputed jurisdiction between the federal government and Maryland. There, on February 7, 1849, in a twilight zone of legality, Sullivan would fight in the first recognized bout for the championship of the world against Tom Hyer, who was 6' 1" and weighed 180 pounds.

This was the era of bare-knuckle fighting, a brutal sport in which the match lasted until one of the contestants was knocked out. A round lasted until one man was knocked down. After a thirty-second rest, the referee called "time" and the fighters had to toe the mark at the center of the ring within eight seconds or forfeit the match. Those were the only rules. Virtually everything else was permitted, including wrestling, choking, and hitting below the belt.

Yankee Sullivan supporters, Irish-Americans all, were on one side of the ring wearing green scarves and flying green banners. Tom Hyer's fans on the other side wore blue scarves and were all native American "blue bloods." Hyer, who had a reputation as a street fighter and enforcer for the Know-Nothing Party, wrestled and fell on Yankee Sullivan repeatedly. After nineteen rounds Sullivan wound up in the hospital. Hyer had done his part in upholding the honor of Protestant America by holding off the Irish in the sport of boxing. Hyer retired undefeated thereafter, but the match was the last stand of the Know-Nothing movement in the world of sports: one by one for the next seventy years the champions would all be Irish Americans.

In the years that followed the Sullivan-Hyer match, Anglo-Saxon fans of the sport were reduced to cheering for an Irishman, as invariably both contestants in major fights would be from Ireland or of Irish-American heritage. Some years later, when he was forty-one, Yankee Sullivan was challenged by a brash upstart called John

Morrissey from County Tipperary. Ironically, Sullivan became the Anglo-Saxon hope even for those in the Know-Nothing movement. He surprised everybody by going thirty-seven rounds against a younger and stronger opponent. In a stormy ending, Sullivan diverted his attention to punch one of Morrissey's seconds, and he failed to toe the mark in time for the next round. The decision went to Morrissey.

The first major international fight in which an Irish-American carried the Stars and Stripes of his adopted country was the one that Currier and Ives called *The Great Fight for the Championship* between the "Benicia Boy," John C. Heenan, and the undisputed champion of England, Tom Sayers. This match took place on April 17, 1860, in Farnborough, Hampshire, England. It had great social significance because it temporarily united American Protestant and Know-Nothing supporters with Irish immigrants against the common foe, England. No sporting event up to that time had captured the imagination of both countries as did this battle for the championship of the world. It was as if the countries were at war and the outcome would be decided by the chosen knights, Heenan and Sayers. England had been the cradle of prize-fighting and the match was viewed as a test of national honor and supremacy. Though prize-fighting was illegal in both countries, the match generated unbridled enthusiasm and excitement on both sides of the Atlantic.

Heenan was born in Troy, New York, a city that would produce three Irish-American world champions and where strong muscles were built by hard labor in the iron mills. He went west at the age of seventeen and worked for the Pacific Mail Steamship Company in Benicia, California, and, though he grew into a 6' 2", two hundred pound adult, he took the name "Benicia Boy." He became an enforcer for a political party in California but, when the going got rough, he departed for New York and joined Tammany Hall, whose leaders knew how to take care of their boys. He was rewarded with a soft job in the customs house.

Once Irish-Americans dominated the boxing scene many of the great fights in subsequent years capitalized on the Irish political struggle by pitting Irish-American fighters against the best that England had to offer. This sentiment peaked in the reign of the great John L. Sullivan, who always fought with the green flag in his corner. Once the fight crowd was so vehemently anti-English that, when John L. went seventy-five rounds against fellow Irish-American Jack Kilrain in Lynchburg, Mississippi in 1889, he tried to label his opponent English because he had a British boxer called Charlie Mitchell in his corner. To many Irish immigrants, the success of their boxing heroes offered proof that with freedom the Irish were every bit as good as the British. These sporting victories gave the people confidence and a view of opportunities for climbing the ladder of success. When the native

Protestant population began to identify with the Irish champions, their popularity helped in absorbing the immigrants into the mainstream of American society.

JOHN C. HEENAN

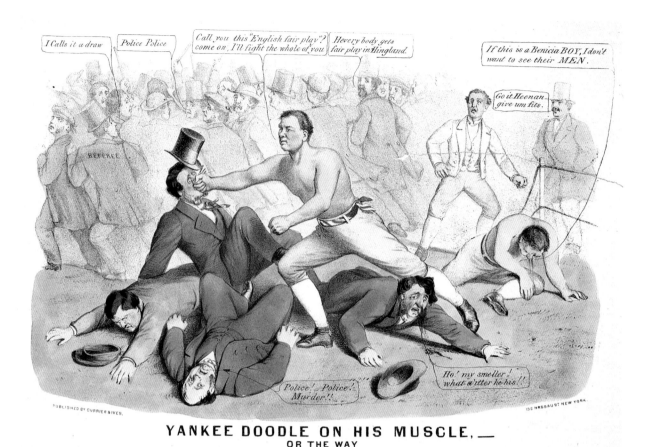

YANKEE DOODLE ON HIS MUSCLE, —
OR THE WAY
The Benicia BOY astonished the English MEN.

YANKEE DOODLE ON HIS MUSCLE
OR THE WAY THE BENICIA BOY ASTONISHED THE ENGLISH MEN

The ending of the great fight almost started a shooting war. After thirty-seven rounds, Heenan had Sayers's head against the ropes. As police and spectators pushed their way into the ring, the referee called the contest a draw. However, a further five rounds ensued, with the audience mixing in with the combatants. The print is not far from the truth in showing how the match ended.

American newspapers were unanimous in claiming that their boy had been cheated. According to them, the match had received such widespread publicity that England could not afford to lose face in the eyes of Europe and the rest of the world. Even *The New York Times* joined the other New York papers in making the accusation that the fight had been stopped on the orders of the British government. This was presumably to prevent Sayers from losing and keep the image of British superiority intact. Either way the myth of English fair play took a severe beating. Ballads were published in America after the fight which mixed history, revolution, and boxing, and praised the victory of Heenan over his opponent. The Irish-Americans sang one:

Attend you sons of Erin, and listen with delight,
To a ditty, 'tis concerning the great and glorious fight,
On the 17th of April, when thousands went with joy,
To see the English champion and the bold Benicia Boy.

The rest of the population had another:

Remember, Uncle Johnnie, the giant stronger grows,
He is always on his muscle, and ready for his foes;
When but a boy at Yorktown, I caused you for to sigh,
So when e'er you boast of fighting, Johnnie Bull,
   mind your eye.

Heenan came home to a hero's welcome throughout the East Coast and was greeted by fifty thousand people at a reception at Jones's Wood Park in New York City. Thereafter, it was downhill all the way. After a few exhibition fights and an inability to make a living as a faro parlor operator, he headed west again for California. He died on the way at Green River, Wyoming, still a "boy" at the age of thirty-nine.

JOHN MORRISSEY

The fight was over a woman in one of the many old saloons that filled New York City's Bowery prior to the Civil War. A tough named McCann, the accuser and aggressor, knocked John Morrissey across a coal stove, scattering the burning embers on the floor. Morrissey was pinned beneath McCann, and the coals were burning the flesh off his back before a sympathetic spectator doused the flames with a bucket of water. Morrissey, who had always demonstrated an incredible ability to take punishment, came back through the steam and smoke to batter his opponent into submission and earn thereafter the title of "Old Smoke."

With his aggressiveness and endurance, it was inevitable that Morrissey would become champion of America some day, but unlike the other bare-knuckle boxers of that time, he had more to offer than big fists. Morrissey not only amassed a personal fortune rivaling that of today's athletic superstars, but also had a successful political career, which included two successive terms as a United States congressman. All in all, not bad for a fellow who could neither read nor write before his twenty-first birthday.

Morrissey was born in Templemore, County Tipperary, in 1831. He was three years old when his family emigrated to Troy, New York. While visiting New York City as a young man, he was almost killed when he took on four men at once in a saloon fight, but a local political leader who saw the action was impressed with his courage and took him under his wing. The Tammany Hall organization groomed Morrissey for two trades that were very useful in the hurly-burly world of New York politics—Immigrant Runner and Shoulder Hitter. As a Runner, he greeted arriving immigrants at the dock, learned what they needed, and found them a place to stay. He also helped them to find jobs, and later found a judge who would grant them citizenship at once. Thus, when they were finally registered to vote, their loyalty to the Tammany political machine was assured. His work as a Shoulder Hitter, on the other hand, was not so pacific: he was called on to use the fighting skills for which he was first noticed. His opponents were the organizers and ward leaders of any competitors to Tammany Hall's dominance, including members of the Know-Nothing Party.

In one of these actions, William Poole, a native-born ward leader of the Know-Nothing Party and friend of the boxing champion Tom Hyer, was shot dead by four men a few hours after a violent argument with Morrissey in a local saloon. There was no evidence to implicate Morrissey other than that the killers were his friends. Charges against him had to be dropped.

In 1851 Morrissey was smitten with gold fever and followed the forty-niners to California. The search for gold was disappointing, however, so he turned to prizefighting to make a living. At one point he challenged George Thompson, a Know-Nothing compatriot of Tom Hyer's, for the championship of California. Morrissey's face was pounded almost beyond recognition in the fight, but he came back to whip Thompson in eleven rounds. He returned to New York with a reputation as an Irishman who could beat almost anyone, including the native-born toughs.

In New York, Tom Hyer evaded a fight with Morrissey, and, as time went by, it became obvious that the only worthy opponent was Yankee Sullivan himself, the old American champion, now forty-one and old enough to be Morrissey's father. Yankee Sullivan, the hometown boy, was the underdog in the contest. For thirty-seven rounds, despite his age, he surprised everybody by getting the better of Morrissey, but in a free-for-all ending, the younger man was declared the winner. In his last fight, Morrissey again took incredible punishment before he beat the "Benicia Boy," John Heenan, and, thereafter, he retired undefeated at the age of thirty.

Retirement was a wise move, since most bare-knuckle fighters never made it past middle age. Morrissey still had many contributions to make, however, and he lived to see all his dreams come true. Before he retired from boxing, he had developed a unique talent in running a faro parlor. Faro was popular among gamblers in that era. Before long he owned a string of fifteen parlors, which in time made him a wealthy man.

He also entered politics and, with the aid of Tammany Hall, became a powerful New York City politician. The recognition he had earned as a heavyweight champion was a valuable asset, which he used to his advantage. In 1864, he built the Saratoga racetrack in upstate New York and, in 1866, he was elected to Congress eventually serving two successive terms. Morrissey had the courage and toughness to oppose Boss Tweed, the leader of Tammany Hall, in 1868, and testified to the corruption of Tweed's organization. When his former supporters opposed him, he defeated their candidates for the state senate in two different terms. Morrissey also conducted benefits for the poor of Ireland while climbing the social ladder. He left his unsavory reputation as a street fighter behind him. When he died in 1878, he was widely respected and admired by all, now a fatherly figure still known as "Old Smoke."

JOHN L. SULLIVAN:
CHAMPION PUGILIST OF THE WORLD

The story of how John L. Sullivan broke into boxing is well known to aficionados of the sport of bare-knuckle prizefighting. As a young man he took up the challenge of a professional named Scannell in front of a big crowd in a Boston theater. Better than merely lasting three rounds, the duration of the challenge, Sullivan promptly sent Scannell through the ropes. Turning to the crowd, he proclaimed, "My name's John L. Sullivan, and I can lick any son of a bitch alive! If any of 'em here doubts it, come on!" There were a few doubters, but they, too, quickly followed Scannell through the ropes.

There were no more takers and John L. became the new braggart on the block in south Boston which, by the miracle of his birth, became the center of the fistic universe. Later in his career, when John L. came home to tell his dad that he was champion of the world, his old man, who came from County Kerry and stood all of 5' 2" tall and weighed 125 pounds, said "Yer nothing, John. There's men in the back hills of Ireland who would break you in two at the snap of a finger." Probably not, but there may have been a few women like his mom, from County Roscommon, who stood 5' 10" tall and weighed in at 190 pounds, the same as her son in full fighting trim when he beat Paddy Ryan for the championship of the world.

Paddy Ryan, "the Trojan Giant" (he was from Troy, New York), was the reigning heavyweight champion when Sullivan burst on the scene. Being a careful fellow who wished to remain champ as long as possible, for he enjoyed the adulation of the pretty opera stars, he avoided an immediate challenge from the upstart Sullivan. "Go and get a reputation," he sneered, knowing full well that John L. already had one.

Sullivan dutifully obeyed, and mowed down every available pugilist in sight, with a nonstop aggressive attack and a punch equivalent to a blow by a telephone pole. But John L. had a quality that made him unlike the other great fighters of those days. Inside that ferocious exterior was the spirit of a child and a heart of gold, which soon began to endear him to the fans. On a barnstorming tour he would offer fifty dollars to anyone who would stay three rounds in the ring with him. He once decked a three-hundred-pound lumberjack and, on noticing the man's wife weeping nearby, he gave her the fifty dollars anyway.

He was a good-natured man who gave without question to every charity and he never went into a saloon, a favorite pastime of his, without buying a round for the house. He also loved the girls and showered them with gifts. In the course of his career, he made a million dol-lars and spent it all. So, when he finally met Paddy Ryan on February 7, 1882 and knocked him out in nine short rounds with his famous "tiger leap," there were none to weep for Paddy. John L. had already won the hearts and minds of the sporting public. With baseball still in its infancy, the only sport that attracted thousands of fans in Currier and Ives's day was prize fighting.

In the Ryan-Sullivan match for the championship of America, both fighters tried to be more American and more Irish than the other. The Stars and Stripes were joined by the Irish harp in each corner. Paddy Ryan went one better by having the sunburst emblem of the revolutionary Fenian Brotherhood on his side. The fight, however, established Sullivan as an American folk hero beloved by all. The Irish, not yet having fully made it in American society, basked in his glory as songs and verses about him proliferated in the media:

> His colors are the stars and stripes
> He also wears the green,
> And he's the grandest slugger that
> The Ring has ever seen
> No fighter in the world can beat
> Our true American,
> The champion of all champions
> Is John L. Sullivan!

He did make one enemy though, an Irishman by the name of Kyle Fox, who was the editor of a racy sports magazine called *Police Gazette*. After his victory, Sullivan refused an invitation to join Fox at the dinner table. Fox was furious and, from then on, virtually every fighter that Sullivan faced in the ring was financed, publicized, and praised by *Police Gazette*. Sullivan, meanwhile, was ridiculed as a slobbering, useless, over-the-hill alcoholic slugger.

Sullivan's nemesis in the ring was a smart, quick young English fighter called Charlie Mitchell. In 1887, five years after he had won the crown, the great but out-of-shape John L. failed to catch Mitchell in thirty-nine muddy rounds at the Baron de Rothschild's estate in France. The fight was declared a draw at the onset of a heavy rainstorm. Win or draw, his reputation was now worldwide, and he was a friend of presidents as well as the future king of England. As the best known private citizen of the world, he was welcomed at an emotional homecoming in Dublin by crowds that rivaled any of those that turned out for the monster meetings of Daniel O'Connell. The fans even knew the Boston greeting, "Shake the hand that shook the hand of John L. Sullivan."

JOHN L. SULLIVAN

PADDY RYAN

Back in America, Kyle Fox proclaimed the crown for-feited, and pronounced Jack Kilrain the new heavyweight champion of the world. Kilrain was, indeed, a formidable fighter. Sullivan, who now made his money in exhibitions with the use of gloves, had adopted the new Marquess of Queensbury rules to stay on the right side of the law and had come to despise the bare-knuckle brawl. But Kilrain had developed a reputation that made him impossible to avoid. Since the sporting world would accept nothing less than a bare-knuckle fight to decide the issue, Sullivan was forced to return to his original style. The fight was memorialized by poet Vachel Lindsay:

Upon an emerald plain
John L. Sullivan
The strong boy
Of Boston
Fought seventy-five rounds with Jack Kilrain.

Though nobody realized it at the time, Sullivan's vic-tory over Kilrain would be the last great bare-knuckle fight of the era. Gentleman Jim Corbett, the up and com-ing fighter who would take the crown from Sullivan, also preferred to fight with gloves. Thus, Sullivan took the bare-knuckle crown of the London Prize Ring rules with him to the grave. Even though Irish-Americans like Cor-bett, Jack Dempsey, and Gene Tunney would continue to dominate the heavyweight division in future decades, Sullivan was the last to carry the green flag of the Irish immigrant in his corner. In his own way, he played a significant part in gaining popularity and acceptance for the Irish immigrant in American society. Different from the role played by Archishop John Hughes, and certainly from that of such prominent activists as Thomas Francis Meagher, Sullivan's was crucial, nevertheless, as the world of Currier and Ives came to a close in the latter part of the nineteenth century.

THE LAND OF RETURN

A trip to Ireland can be like a time-travel experience. This can be true for returning immigrants, for those of Irish descent who have never been there, or for first-time visitors with no connection to the place. Irish-Americans by and large have a mental picture of the people and the country that has been passed down to them from older generations.

Some of these pictures have been reinforced by the occasional movie that includes rural scenes of Cork, Wicklow, Connemara, the lakes of Killarney, or the Aran Islands. They reinforce the image of a wild and mystical land. Even Dublin is often viewed as a quaint but unreal place, peopled by writers and revolutionaries. The images presented by Currier and Ives late in the last century helped to perpetuate the view of a beautiful land and a simpler time. It is embedded in the collective memory of the diaspora. For the vast majority of the forty-four million Americans who claim Irish heritage and will never visit Ireland it remains quaint and unchanging.

In the real Ireland, the old is, indeed, often preserved alongside the new, so that even in the city of Dublin, now home to a million people, the landmarks of Currier and Ives days are still there to be seen. There is no question that Ireland has developed less quickly than many other countries. This is due to its geographical location on the periphery of Europe, as well as to centuries of English political and economic oppression.

For a visitor of Irish descent, an attempt to find roots in the old country may indeed be an adventure in time travel, because in many cases scenes pictured in the old Currier and Ives prints are virtually unchanged since they were drawn by the engravers of the nineteenth century. One can take out a camera on the bridge across the River Nore and capture a view of Kilkenny Castle almost identical to that seen by the artist who drew it for Currier and Ives. Admittedly, the print does not show Kilkenny Town, with the fancy boutiques, antiques shops, restaurants, and pubs that now completely surround the Castle. These are now crowded with well-dressed local customers as well as international tourists. Still, Kilkenny, like some other towns in Ireland, with its narrow and unplanned streets, alleyways, and overhangs, captivates travelers so that they can feel they have gone back to an earlier time. High-rise office buildings and shopping malls have still not penetrated.

In the countryside, places pictured by Currier and Ives such as Rostrevor, the Killeries, the Old Weir Bridge (a realistic view), and the lakes of Killarney are also still largely unchanged. But as beautiful as castles, lakes, and mountains may be, no trip to the old country for an Irish-American would be complete without a visit to Cobh. This once-bustling seaport was known as the Cove of Cork to the Irish and as Queenstown to the English. Cobh saw the vast majority of immigrants set sail to America for decades before the Statue of Liberty was there to welcome them, before Ellis Island was ready to receive them, and indeed all the way up to the 1960s. Then, air travel relegated Cobh to a quaint backwater, but it will always live in the collective memory of those it sent onward to new lives in the New World.

Opposite:
HOMEWARD BOUND

Next pages:
DUBLIN BAY

Just a few years ago a Viking longboat was excavated in Denmark. The entire wooden ship, still virtually intact, was examined microscopically by scholars to determine its mission and origin. The scientific community was startled to learn that the ship had been constructed in Dublin in A.D. 1050, some forty years after the Vikings had been defeated at the Battle of Clontarf by BrianBorú.

The discovery of the Viking ship proved what was already known in Ireland, that many defeated warriors had settled down to become traders and good local citizens, eventually converting to Christianity and intermarrying with the native Dubliners to form a new race of people called Ostmen.

A hundred years later, the English, under Henry II, would succeed the Vikings in dominating Dublin Bay, a natural harbor shaped like an open mouth facing the Irish Sea that separates the two countries. As it had been under the pillaging Vikings, Dublin once again became a center of foreign civilization in Ireland and the city, together with a small area around it, became known as the Pale. The rest of the country, not quite suppressed or civilized and which included such places as Clonmacnoise, the Rock of Cashel, and Saint Patrick's Seat at Armagh, lay Beyond the Pale, an expression that many people use today without knowing its meaning.

As English influence spread out Beyond the Pale, Dublin grew to rival London as the second city of the empire. In the eighteenth century, under the leadership of its cosmopolitan Anglo-Irish elite, magnificent Georgian mansions and decorative squares such as St. Stephen's Green were constructed. The city produced such noted writers as Jonathan Swift, Edmund Burke, Oliver Goldsmith, and George Berkeley, as well as one of England's greatest military leaders, the Duke of Wellington.

Dublin's cosmopolitanism declined after the Act of Union with Britain, when the Irish parliament was dissolved and all the peers and members of their entourages then spent the annual lawmaking season in London. By the time the Currier and Ives print was drawn, the city already had an air of stagnation, with little commerce to enrich it. As the limited boat and steamer activity in the print suggests, Dublin remained the capital of a rural country that experienced few of the benefits of the Industrial Revolution.

Many of Dublin's landmarks are still discernible in this old print. On the top right, the Isthmus of Howth juts out into the sea; the Bailey Lighthouse is visible at its tip. Clontarf, where Daniel O'Connell's monster meeting was called off, is on the left of the print just within the bay enclosure. On the narrow sliver of land above sits Poolbeg Lighthouse. To the right of the enclosure is Dun Laoghaire, and if you follow the row of houses on the water to the extreme right of the print you can see the martello tower at Sandycove. It was there that Stephen Dedalus and Buck Mulligan took up abode in James Joyce's extraordinary novel *Ulysses*.

Dublin came to the fore in the struggle for Irish independence in 1916. Eamon De Valera from America, James Connolly, born in Ireland but raised in Scotland, and Anglo-Irishman Patrick Pearse, with six hundred members of the Irish Volunteers, seized Dublin's public buildings, including the post office. They proclaimed a free Ireland, knowing full well that the English, cheered on by the Dublin crowds would, if necessary, level the city in order to get them. And level some of it they did: two hundred houses were destroyed. The rebellion failed, but it became a cleansing experience for the residents of the city, forcing them to reexamine who they were and what kind of future they wanted for their city and country. They decided to embrace the defeated Volunteers and joined the struggle, echoing William Butler Yeats's oft-quoted lines:

> All changed, changed utterly,
> A terrible beauty is born.

The Cove of Cork

The Cove of Cork is a small city on a beautiful bay which leads into Cork Harbor. Cork itself is the third city of Ireland after Dublin and Belfast. The city was renamed Queenstown after a visit by Queen Victoria in 1848, and it remained Queenstown until independence in 1922. At that time its Gaelic name, Cobh, was reinstated. Historically, Cobh has been both the gateway to Ireland and, together with nearby Kinsale, its path of invasion from the sea. Both these cities today maintain their eighteenth-century ambience.

Cobh has also signaled the theme of Outward Bound, since political prisoners at the time of Cromwell were sent from there to Jamaica, Barbados, and particularly Montserrat, the Emerald Isle of the Caribbean. Later, prisoners were shipped from Cobh to Tasmania. It is estimated that 20 percent of the present population of Australia is descended from these political prisioners. As the famine broke out in Ireland in the early 1840s, the beginnings of a vast exodus were funneled from Dublin, Cobh, and other ports to Canada and the United States.

One can visit Cobh today and still see the view in the Currier and Ives print. It is spoiled only by the Irish Steel plant, which sits by the left side of Haulbowline Island, pictured in the foreground. The buildings of the British naval base remain virtually untouched and unchanged. Only the flag of occupation is gone. Now the Tricolor, the flag of the Irish Republic, flies over what is now an Irish naval station. The small island at the left foreground of the print is Spike Island, which houses the British prison where, in 1848, John Mitchel was held after being sentenced to fourteen years servitude for his publication of the newspaper The *United Irishman*.

A close examination of the large sailing boat in the left foreground clearly shows that it is flying the American flag and appears to be a naval vessel. The cottage pictured is gone, but there is a small museum near the site which preserves memories of this beautiful and historic place.

The scenery of County Cork is featured in a number of other Currier and Ives prints, including *The Cork River, Near Glanmire,* and *Cromwell's Bridge, Glengariff.*

THE YACHT "DAUNTLESS" OF NEW YORK
OFF QUEENSTOWN, IRELAND, JULY 13, 1869

In his diary, the *Jail Journal,* the patriot John Mitchel describes the queen's historic visit to Cobh (Queenstown) while he was on board a convict ship awaiting transportation to Bermuda. He is barely able to restrain himself and his biting sarcasm is at its best:

This year Her Majesty's Advisors deemed the coast clear for the Royal Yacht. Plenty of blazing, vociferous excitement called "loyalty". Loyalty, you are to know, consists of a willingness to come out into the street to see a pageant pass. Besides, the visit was most happily timed; the "additional powers" would not expire for a month yet. Habeas Corpus still in suspension; jails still yawning for seditious persons; Lord Clarendon still wielding his Lettres De Cachet. No happier combination of circumstances could be imagined; so her gracious Majesty has come and enthroned herself in the hearts of her Irish Subjects; and the newspapers are to say (at their peril) that a brighter day is just going to dawn for Ireland. . . . The newspaper I have seen says the Queen met with nothing but loyalty; and that "Young Ireland was no where to be seen." . . . Her Majesty did not visit Spike Island . . . Her Majesty did not visit Skibbereen, Westport, or Scull [very poor areas where the potato famine had taken a terrible toll and people were dying of starvation on the side of the roads]. Neither did she "drop in" as sometimes in Scotland to dine with any of the peasantry, on their "homely fare". After a few years, however, it is understood that Her Majesty will visit the West.

The human inhabitants are expected by that time, to have been sufficiently thinned, and the deer and other game to have proportionately multiplied. The Prince Albert will then take a hunting lodge in Connemara.

The first yachting club in the world, the Royal Cork Yacht Club, was founded at Cobh in 1854 by wealthy Anglo-Irishmen. Housed in a beautiful Italianate villa at the water's edge, it has been restored today as the Sirius Center for the Arts. The yacht shown here, *Dauntless*, an American boat, arrived off Queenstown in 1869 in its race across the Atlantic to New York. Cork was later visited by the Shamrock series of yachts built in Ireland and owned by the tea industrialist Thomas Lipton, who tried five times and failed to win the America's Cup at the turn of the century. One of these yachts is still preserved at Newport, Rhode Island.

CROMWELL'S BRIDGE, GLENGARIFF

THE KILLERIES—CONNEMARA

The print shows the fjord-like entrance to Killery Bay between the counties of Mayo and Galway on the Atlantic Ocean. At the time Currier and Ives made this picture, Killery was home to a fishing industry of small curragh boats that thrived on the abundant herring shoals in these waters. At times, the herring would disappear for years only to reappear abruptly, perhaps ten years later, more numerous than before. A tax on salt forced fishermen to sell their catch quickly, before it spoiled, keeping fish cheap and fishermen poor.

The Sea of Connemara is a cruel one. Some of the ships that survived the Spanish Armada came to ruin here. The power of the sea and its effect on the people who eked out a living on these shores were told hauntingly by J. M. Synge in his classic one-act play *Riders to the Sea*. In the play Maurya, an old woman, mourns the death of her last son:

> It's little the likes of him knows of the sea—Bartley will be lost now, and let you call Eamon and make me a good coffin out of the white boards, for I won't live after them. I've had a hus-band, and a husband's father and six sons in this house—six fine men, though it was a hard birth I had with every one of them and they coming to the world—and some of them were found and some of them were not found, but they're gone now—the lot of them . . . There was Stephen, and Shawn, were lost in the great wind and found after in the Bay of Gregory of the Golden Mouth, and carried up the two of them on the one plank and in by that door . . . There was Sheamus and his father and his own father again, were lost in a dark night, and not a stick or sign was seen of them when the sun went up. There was Patch after was drowned out of a curragh that turned over . . . They're all gone now and there isn't any-thing more the sea can do to me.

The fishermen of Killery passed their skills and knowledge down from father to son but they never learned to swim. Today, there is a youth hostel in this beautiful place to accommodate adventurous tourists and a modern shell-fishing industry that gives some employ-ment to local residents.

THE LAKES OF KILLARNEY

Currier and Ives published a number of romantic views of the lakes and hills around a small village in Ireland called Killarney, a name that has become virtually synonymous with the scenic beauty of the country as a whole. Several of these prints are reproduced in the first section of this book. Harry T. Peters, whose fine collection of Currier and Ives prints is now the property of the Museum of the City of New York, comments on this scene: "One print, *The Lakes of Killarney*, is a graphic view, full of detail, and one of the best landscapes issued by Currier and Ives."

Currier and Ives, who always gave the customers what they wanted, printed at least sixteen different views of the Killarney region. With the exception of New York City, there are more views of Killarney than any other place, including anywhere else in the United States.

Kilkenny Castle stands today as an imposing and well-preserved structure, as it did when the print was made, and as it has for some eight hundred years. Built in the twelfth century, it remains a monument to the Norman invasion of Ireland, and for some five hundred years it was the home of the Butlers. This family included both Catholics and Protestants, but they rarely, if ever, made the mistake of being loyal to Ireland. Just about the only thing Ireland can thank them for is the preservation of the magnificent castle, which, in its own way, remains Ireland's answer to the Palace of Versailles.

The family's original name was Walter. The astute Theobold Walter managed to get himself appointed by the King of England as "Chief Butler of Ireland," a title that made him a senior toastmaster at the coronation banquet, where he offered the new king his first cup of wine. Because of this, the family took the name Butler. Their ability to please royalty and to survive in the process was amply demonstrated by the way they showed their loyalty to Prince Charles, son of King Charles I, who had been executed by parliamentary forces under the leadership of the Puritan Oliver Cromwell.

Cromwell approached Kilkenny in 1650 and his cannons battered the south wall of the castle (not shown in the print). It is probable that he sent the Butlers his usual note in such circumstances:

Sirs,

Having brought the army and my cannon near this place according to my usual manner in summoning places, I thought fit to offer you terms honourable to soldiers; that you may march away with your baggage, arms and colours, free from injuries or violence. But if I'd be, notwithstanding, necessitated to bend my cannon further upon you, you must expect the extremity usual in such cases. To avoid blood, this is offered to you.

Your Servant,
Oliver Cromwell

James Butler, 12th Earl of Ormond, aware of the devastation Cromwell was inflicting on those who were resisting his invasion, marched away, going into exile with Prince Charles. Lady Butler, however, claimed that the castle and its lands were really hers and not that of her treacherous husband and convinced Cromwell to let her keep the estate despite her husband's treason. After Cromwell's death in 1660, the monarchy was restored, Charles II returned triumphantly to England with his "butler," and James Butler returned to Ireland more powerful than before.

In the last years of the seventeenth century another James Butler proved just as slick as his predecessor. By joining the cause of King William of Orange who had defeated the Irish forces at the Battle of the Boyne (see page 33), he again assured that Kilkenny would remain in Butler hands.

In the nineteenth century, when the Currier and Ives print was drawn, the Butlers were typical of the landed gentry, serving in the British army and running a vast estate of impoverished tenants who paid high rents for their small plots of land. During the potato famine, those who could not pay their rents were evicted. The lucky ones who could raise the fare escaped to the New World, where many would keep the name of their oppressor, Butler. Others traveled the roads facing death from disease and starvation.

The Butlers' luck was to hold right up to 1922. Then the castle was occupied by the more nationalist faction of the IRA, who were evicted a few days later by the faction that organized the Irish Free State, which later became the Republic of Ireland. A republican and free Ireland, however, was not to the Butlers' liking, as it became clear that the days of kings and queens and dukes and duchesses were over for Ireland. The Butlers auctioned off the contents of the castle in 1935 and left the country. In 1967, Arthur Butler, still calling himself the 24th Earl of Ormond (the old Gaelic name for the province of Munster) sold Kilkenny Castle to a government office, the Castle Restoration Committee, for fifty Irish pounds. Today it is taken care of by the National Parks and Monuments Services of the Office of Public Works and is open to the public. Basking in its restored opulence has become one of Ireland's premier tourist attractions.

KILKENNY CASTLE

NOTES ON COLLECTING
CURRIER AND IVES
IRISH-AMERICAN PRINTS

For the collector, many questions relating to Currier and Ives Irish-American prints remain unanswered. We do not know, for example, how many different Irish subject prints were made, how many copies of each were sold, or how many are preserved today. It is believed that Currier and Ives made about seven thousand prints of different subjects, but the exact figure changes from year to year as additional ones are discovered. The author has identified 204 prints dealing with Irish and Irish-American subjects (see page 133 for complete list) though there may be a few others not yet chronicled or still hidden in attics around the country.

As to the numbers of Currier and Ives Irish-American prints sold, we can only give a rough estimate based on their total output of all prints, which was between two and three million. This would put the number of Irish prints sold in the area of 100,000. More complicated is the question of how many copies of each print subject were sold. For some subjects there are many copies still in existence, while others are difficult, if not impossible, to find. Edition size and rarity are questions that may never be answered in the case of these prints.

Currier and Ives also published prints of scenes in Scotland, England, and Germany, but in nothing like the quantity of prints published on Ireland and Irish-related subjects. Curiously, although the majority of Currier and Ives prints are of American subjects and they are frequently exhibited, it is rare that an exhibition of Currier and Ives features any prints on foreign subject matter. No Irish-American institution has documented the prints that are the focus of this book, nor has any group made an effort to preserve them. The author has collected seventy-five prints, which I believe to be by far the largest group of its kind in existence. I am aware of a few other people who have five or six prints in their collections. The American Irish Historical Society, on Fifth Avenue in New York City, has a magnificent collection of antique Irish history books, but only three Currier and Ives prints. The Irish-American Museum in East Durham, New York, is too new to have much in its own collection, though it is capable of putting on excellent presentations of Irish-American memorabilia.

My discovery of the Currier and Ives Irish-American prints was more or less accidental. Over the years, I reluctantly followed my wife on her occasional visits to antiques shows or an antiques shop. While browsing in an old print shop in Newport, Rhode Island, I discovered some Irish and Irish-American scenes in an 1860s edition of *Harpers' Magazine*. I became interested in the Irish involvement in the American Civil War and began buying these old journals, usually for about $15 or $20. Some time later, while browsing through Currier and Ives prints at an antiques show in White Plains, New York, looking for Civil War generals with Irish names, I discovered something I never knew existed: two Currier and Ives prints on Irish topics, *The Siege of Limerick* and *The Battle of the Boyne*. The print of *The Battle of the Boyne* had a somewhat familiar look to me, until I remembered a popular engraving of Irish history that I had known as a schoolboy. The brilliant colors of *The Siege of Limerick* captivated me. I bought them both, my first collected works of art, paying $85 for *The Boyne* and $160 for *The Siege*.

I later found a guide to Currier and Ives prints by Craig McClain that lists the estimated prices of all known Currier and Ives prints. I saw that my *Boyne* print was only worth $40, while *The Siege* was listed at $45. At first I thought I had not made a very good deal, but soon discovered that collecting art is not like buying necessities. The pleasure I got from the two prints was proving to be well worth the seemingly high prices I had paid for them. A year or so later, while studying McClain's work in more detail, I found that many more Irish titles existed. Still later I discovered that Gale Research of Detroit had published a catalogue raisonne of Currier and Ives prints, giving their publishing histories and their present locations in public and private collections that have made their holdings known.

A novice quickly learns that buying old prints is a complicated, although exhilarating, process. While traveling for business or pleasure, I always try to look in on print shops to see if they have any of the subjects in which I am interested. Many print shops have only a widely varied inventory, but there are specialized dealers who carry quite large numbers of Currier and Ives prints. I have found that in most collections of Currier and Ives prints of fifty or more, there may, however, be only one or two dealing with Irish or Irish-American subjects. And fifty Currier and Ives prints would be considered a major inventory for any shop or dealer who specializes in them. In addition to visiting print dealers one also has to read the various antiques trade journals that list prints for auction. It is possible, then, to try to buy a print by attending the auction or by making a telephone bid.

I was able to assemble my collection because I discovered that the Irish prints were relatively inexpensive. Most of mine were purchased for less than $150. I sometimes found them for much less than that, though none of the prices were as low as those listed in McClain's book. Happily, Irish prints turned out to be cheaper than prints of similar quality in the general field of Americana, which sell for $600 or more. Exceptions to this rule are the prints of early Irish-American boxers such the great John L. Sullivan, Gentleman Jim Corbett, or John Heenan, whose higher prices reflect their status as general American folk heroes. So, while you might pick up a portrait of Daniel O'Connell for $85 to $100, one of John L. Sullivan could go as high as $750. It took this collector five years to find a John L. Sullivan for sale at an affordable price, and I have not yet come across a reasonably priced print of Gentleman Jim Corbett or Paddy Ryan.

The most expensive Currier and Ives print I have ever seen is a large folio print called *Life of a Hunter: A Tight Fix*. It shows a hunter with a knife attempting to defend himself against a huge black bear. This print, not an Irish-American subject, recently sold at auction for $62,000. Overall, Irish-American prints are still a bargain. With limited resources, but a keen interest and a dogged determination, the author accumulated most of the collection depicted on these pages. For the book, to illustrate those images that I do not own, I have obtained photographs for reproduction from the picture departments of The Library of Congress, The New York Public Library, and the Metropolitan Museum of Art.

The best sources of Currier and Ives prints are the six specialized dealers listed in the back of this book. These dealers advertise in the antiques trade journals and publish quarterly price lists of their prints for sale. For the most part, these prices are not negotiable, but they are usually reasonable so haggling is not necessary. Items on display at shows or in shops that do not regularly handle these prints are generally overpriced. Not having full knowledge of the field, these dealers only see the Currier and Ives name and may, thus, set a price two to three times a print's actual value. Further, these prints are rarely, if ever, in good condition.

The least expensive way to buy prints is at auction. This is where dealers purchase most of their prints. It may, however, make more economic sense for a collector to buy directly from a dealer, since hotel and travel costs involved in attending auctions are likely to exceed any savings. Tracking down Currier and Ives Irish scenes or other specialized subjects involves some detective work.

First, go through the trade magazines that list print auctions and check to see if Currier and Ives material is included. Then call the auction house to discover if any of the Currier and Ives prints up for sale has an Irish theme. You should then study some price-list books to help you decide what to bid for the print. If the auction is further away than you wish to travel, it is possible to bid by telephone. When you have decided what you want, call the auctioneer a day or two before the event and make your bid; all the auction house needs is a credit card number. The only risk in buying a print by telephone, however, is that since you have not seen it, you may be disappointed by the print's condition when it is shipped to you.

A good reason to buy from established dealers is that they will never knowingly sell you a print that is not an authentic Currier and Ives. Reproductions are numerous and at most antiques shops or shows the buyer buys at his own risk. Reputable dealers and auction houses, however, will take back material that is not genuine. Fortunately, reproductions of Currier and Ives Irish-American scenes are rare. The only one that I have come across is *Erin Go Bragh*. In 1992 the Travelers Insurance Company printed, perhaps for the first time, an Irish scene entitled *Kilkenny Castle* in their Currier and Ives calendar, and I anticipate that this photomechanical reproduction may show up in antiques shops in the future.

McClain's book is helpful to the novice in determining whether a Currier and Ives is an original or a reproduction. If you stick to Irish scenes, reproductions will not be much of a factor, but if you stray into the broad area of Currier and Ives much more care is required. Because of their particular interest in Currier and Ives and their maintenance of relatively large inventories, the six major dealers have unwittingly made an important contribution in preserving the Irish-American heritage. They will save any print, even of an obscure Irish subject, if it has the Currier and Ives label.

When I travel, I look through the yellow pages for dealers in old prints and seek them out. Thus, for example, on a visit to New Orleans in 1990, I walked into a print shop in the French Quarter and was greeted by the picture of General Corcoran on his white horse leading his Irish brigade in the Civil War. The owner told me that for years he couldn't get any Southerner to buy this picture of a Yankee general. In five years of collecting I had never seen this rare and beautiful print for sale. I was ecstatic with the price of $175, and so was the dealer, since he never thought he would sell it.

Tracking down some of these prints, however, can only be described as a labor of love. The hidden costs can sometimes be astronomical. I acquired the print *Saint Patrick* in Atlantic City on March 18, 1989, but not until I had tramped over seven and a half acres of concessions at a monster antique show and put in two nights at a motel. The print was priced at $130, but with the aid of McClain's book—which listed the print at $45—I was able to negotiate the dealer down to $80 and the bargain was made.

It takes years of experience to evaluate a reasonable price for a Currier and Ives print, despite the proliferation of price guides on the subject. As noted above, however, the enjoyment that prints provide can be priceless. It is well to note that most collectors will sell prints, and it is always valuable, therefore, to ask fellow collectors if they have a print you are especially eager to own. It may be that they have more than one copy or are willing to part with a print because there is something else they desire more. At first, when I began collecting, I was under the impression that I was the only person in the United States collecting these prints. That proved not to be the case, but I have yet to meet a collector willing to go to such extremes to locate a print. Over the years, I have learned not to pass up an Irish print regardless of its condition because I might never find it again.

To me, the most interesting prints are those that show Irish life in the old country. At the time they were issued, these scenes were not all that popular; the immigrants did not want to be reminded of the conditions they left behind. As a result very few of them were sold, and they are consequently very scarce today. Such prints include *Auld Times at Donnybrook Fair, Paddy Murphy's Jantin Car, Paddy and the Pigs,* and *Outward Bound.* The most popular prints seem to be those about Killarney, Kilkenny Castle, the Vale of Avoca, and the Cove of Cork. Also popular are the prints showing the Irish in the Civil War, though this author has never been able to track down the print called *Thomas Francis Meagher at Fredericksburg.* I would also value highly those prints involving the Revolution of 1848: the American Irish Historical Society has a copy of *The Trial of Irish Patriots at Clonmel,* but I have never seen it for sale. The same holds true for *Attack on the Widow McCormack's House* and *Signal Fires On The Slievenamon Mountains.*

As I mentioned previously, prints showing the bare-knuckle fighters of Irish-American heritage command a premium price. I would assume that they exist in private collections, though I have rarely seen any of them for sale. In years of collecting, I have never come across *Paddy Ryan—The Trojan Giant* or *James J. Corbett—Champion Heavyweight,* nor do they exist in any collection or museum of which I am aware. (The copy of the *Paddy Ryan* that we show is a reproduction of the print.) Yet these two fighters were immensely popular in their time, and many such prints must have been sold. They may still turn up at an auction at any time.

As my collection progressed, I came to appreciate the fact that this treasure of Irish-American history was being inadvertently preserved, but never discovered by others. This book is an attempt to share that discovery with Irish America. This art is a truly priceless part of their heritage. It shows that the immigrants brought their heroes with them, kept the beautiful buildings and landscapes of home on their walls in America, and carried Ireland for generations in their hearts.

A LIST OF DEALERS

Bob Bascom Prints
Box 4334
Burlington, VT 05406
802-893-4082

George Cohenour
4301 Beaumont Road
Dover, PA 17315
717-292-5345

Robert B. Kipp
16 Wedgemere Road
Beverly, MA 01915-1435
508-922-6852

Rudisill's Alt Print Haus
P.O. Box 199
Worton, MD 21678
410-778-9290

Robert L. Searjeant
P.O. Box 23942
Rochester, NY 14692
716-424-2489

Robert Wieland
33 S. St. Andrews Dr.
Ormond Beach, FL 32174
904-672-9972

LIST OF 204 IRISH-AMERICAN PRINTS BY CURRIER AND IVES AND HOW TO FIND THEM

LIST OF ABBREVIATIONS

(Note: some prints are not available in any known collection but may be in the hands of private collectors.)

The designation C means that the print is listed in the illustrated check list of Currier and Ives prints compiled by Frederic A. Conningham . The G means that it is listed in the Currier and Ives prints compiled by the Gale Research Company.

AC	Author's Collection
BA	Boston Athenaeum
CHS	Chicago Historical Society
DIA	Detroit Institute of Art
GC	Billy Graham Center (Wheaton, Illinois)
LC	Library of Congress (Washington, D.C.)
LLIU	Lily Library, Indiana University (Bloomington)
MCNY	Museum of the City of New York, Peters Collection
MMA	Metropolitan Museum of Art (New York City)
NYHS	New York Historical Society (New York City)
NYPL	New York Public Library (New York City)
PMA	Philadelphia Museum of Art
RIHS	Rhode Island Historical Society (Providence)
RMA	John and Mable Ringling Museum of Art (Sarasota, Florida)
SI	Smithsonian Institution, National Museum of American Art and National Museum of American History (Washington, D.C.)

Note: In the following list the titles of Currier and Ives prints are given as they appear on the margins of the prints themselves. It should be noted that the punctuation and spelling are inconsistent from print to print and sometimes place and other names are incorrect: the print *Ross Trevor,* for example, refers to the town of Rostrevor in County Down; the print *Rapids of Dunass* refers to the locality of Doonas; the print of a scene from Dion Boucicault's play *The Shaughran* gives the title as "Shaughaun;" the print of the signal fires on Slievnamon Mountain, where Thomas Meagher gave his stirring speech, refers to "mountains," and there are no others. Since Currier and Ives made more than one print of some popular subjects the author has tried to give identifying differences in brackets following each title. Descriptions in parentheses are as given by Currier and Ives.

1. The Abbey of Clare Galway: (Ireland)–C-3, G-0003, AC
2. The Abbey of the Holy Cross: Tipperary, Ireland–C-4, G-0004, AC
3. The Ancient Cross–Clonmacnoise, Ireland–C-215, G-0228
4. The Apostle of Ireland St. Patrick: Born A.D. 372, Died A.D. 464–G-0268, AC
5. Aptommas' History of the Harp–G-0272, LC
6. Attack on the Widow McCormack's House: On Boulagh Common Ireland, July 29th 1848–C-304, G-0325, LC
7. Ballynahinch: Ireland–C-351, G-0385, LC, MCNY
8. The Battle of Clontarf, A.D. 1014: Ireland–C-399, G-0442
9. Battle of the Boyne, July 1st 1690 [horse trotting]– AC
10. Battle of the Boyne: July 1st, 1690 [horse galloping]–C-431, G-0483, MCNY, AC
11. Beauties of Irish Scenery/The Old Weir Bridge, Lakes of Killarney–AC
12. Belted Will's Tower: Naworth, Ireland–C-497, G-0559
13. Black Rock Castle: Cork River, Ireland–C-557, G-0625
14. Blarney Castle: County Cork–C-564, G-0629
15. The Body of the Most Revd. Archbishop Hughes Lying in State: At St. Patrick's Cathedral, N.Y. January 1864–C-585, G-0651, LC, LLIU
16. The Body of the Most Revd. Archbishop Hughes

Lying in State: Before the High Altar of St. Peter's in Rome, February 12, 1864 with His Guard of Honor, from the Noble Guard—C-583, G-0653

17. The Boyne Water—C-642, G-0716, LC, AC
18. Brian Borue: At the Battle of Clontarf—C-656, G-073
18a. Brian Boroimhe: Monarch of Ireland and Hero of Clontarf—AC
19. Brig. Genl. Michael Corcoran: At the Head of His Gallant Irish Brigade—C-680, G-0762, CHS, MCNY, AC
20. Brig. Genl. Michael Corcoran: of the Irish Brigade Late Colonel of the Gallant N.Y. "Sixty Ninth"—C-681, G-0763, LC
21. Brig. Genl. Thomas Francis Meagher, Irish Brigade—C-684, G-0766, AC
22. Capt. Thomas Francis Meagher: Zouave Corps of the "Sixty Ninth"—C-799, G-0893
23. The Castle Blarney, Ireland—C-839, G-0932
24. Castle Howard: Vale of Avoca—C-841, G-0934
25. Catherine Hayes: The Swan of Erin—C-852, G-0945
26. Champion Irish Setter Rover—C-965, G-1059, MCNY, SI
27. Charles Gavin Duffy/"Educate that you may be free"—C-1007, G-1001, LC
28. Charles Stuart Parnell, M.P./The Great Land Agitator. President of the Irish Land League—C-1007, G-1105
29. Charles Stuart Parnell, M.P./President of the Irish Land League, Addressing a Meeting—C-1008, G-1004, LC
30. Col. James A. Mulligan/of the Illinois "Irish Brigade"—C-1197, G-1313, LC, AC
31. Col. John O'Mahoney: Head Center of the Fenian Brotherhood—C-1196, G-1315, AC
32. Col. Michael Corcoran, at the Battle of Bull Run—July 21st 1861: The Desperate and Bloody Charge of the "Gallant Sixty-Ninth," on the Rebel Batteries—C-1199, G-1318, LC, AC
33. Col. Michael Corcoran: Commanding the Sixty-Ninth (Irish) Regiment —C-1200, G-1317, MCNY
34. Coolun: A Favorite Irish Air [music sheet]—G-1368
35. The Cork Castle and Black Rock Castle, Ireland—C-1253, G-1375
36. The Cork River: Near Glanmire, County Cork, Ireland—C-1254, G-1376, AC
37. The Cove of Cork—C-1276, AC
38. The Cove of Cork: Presented to the Lady Patron of McGill & Strong's Mirror of Ireland—G-1398, LC, MCNY
39. The Crack Shots in Position: Dollymount, Creedmore and Wimbledon—C-1280, G-1403, LC, MCNY
40. Cromwell's Bridge: Glengariff, Ireland—C-1303, G-1425, AC
41. Daniel O'Connell: The Champion of Freedom (#164)—C-1356, G-1481, AC

42. Daniel O'Connell: The Champion of Freedom—C-1357, G-1479, LC, AC
43. Daniel O'Connell: The Champion of Freedom (#724)—C-1358, G-1483, AC
44. Daniel O'Connell: The Champion of Freedom (Born Aug. 6th 1775. Died May 15, 1847.)—C-1359, G-1480, LC
45. Daniel O'Connell: The Champion of Freedom [drawn by permission from the large plate pub. by Turner & Fisher]—C-1360, G-1482
46. Daniel O'Connell: The Great Irish "Liberator" and Champion of the Catholic Emancipation—C-1361, G-1484, CHS, AC
47. The "Dargle" Glen: County Wicklow Ireland—C-1367, G-1491, AC
48. The "Dargle" Glen: Ireland—G-1492
49. Darrynane Abbey—Ireland: The Home of O'Connell—C-1445, G-1570, LC
50. The Daughter of Erin—C-1449, G-1573
51. Death of Daniel O'Connell: At Genoa, Saturday May 15th 1847 (His heart in Rome, his body in Ireland, and his soul in Heaven)—C-1479, G-1607, LC
52. Death of St. Patrick, the Apostle of Ireland: At the Monastery of Saul in Ulida, March 17th A.D. 465, Aged 78 years—C-1505, G-1636, CHS, LC
53. The Democracy in Search of a Candidate [a political cartoon including Miles O'Reilly]—C-1550, G-1683, CHS, LC, NYPL
54. The Devil's Glen: Killarney, Ireland—C-1574, G-1709
55. Disloyal British "Subject"—C-1586, G-1723, BA, LC
56. Dublin Bay: From Kingston Quarries—G-1770
57. Dublin Bay: Ireland—C-1631, G-1771
58. Dublin Bay Ireland: From Kingston Quarries—C-1632, G-1772, LC
59. Dublin Bay, Ireland: From Kingston Quarries—G-1773, AC
60. Emmet's Betrothed—C-1731, G-1876, MCNY, AC
61. Erin Go Bragh: The Great International Rifle Match, Dollymount, July 1875—C-1753, G-1899, LC, AC [This print is companion to non-Irish subject prints entitled *E. Pluribus Unum*, *The Highland Fling*, and *The Queen's Own*.]
62. The Fair Rose of Killarney: Ballad of Miss Eliza Cook, the Music by Stephen Glover [music sheet]—G-1969, LC, AC
63. Father Matthew: Administering the Temperance Pledge—C-1913, G-2077
64. Father Matthew Administering the Temperance Pledge "May God Bless You and Enable You to Keep Your Promise"—C-1914, G-2078, MCNY
65. The Fenian Volunteer—C-1940, G-2107
66. Freedom to Ireland—C-2136, G-2310, LC

67. The Funeral of Daniel O'Connell, Thursday Aug 5, 1847. The Hearse passing Mr. O'Connell's House in Merrion Square—C-2205, G-2388, LC, MCNY, AC

68. Gallant Charge of the "Sixty-Ninth": On the Rebel Batteries at the Battle of Bull Run, VA., July 21st, 1861—C-2213, G-2398, MCNY

69. Gallant Charge of the "Sixty-Ninth" On the Rebel Batteries at the Battle of Bull Run, VA., July 21, 1861—RIHS, AC

70. The Gap of Dunloe: Ireland—C-2219, G-2404, AC

71. Genl. Meagher at the Battle of Fair Oaks Va. June 1st 1862—C-2289, G-2514, LC, MCNY, AC

72. Genl. Meagher at the Battle of Fair Oaks, Va. June 1st 1862—G-2515, AC

73. Genl. Thomas Francis Meagher at the Battle of Fredricksburg, Va. Dec. 13, 1862—C-2301, G-2522

74. The Giant's Causeway: County Antrim, Ireland—C-2372, G-2575, AC

75. Glengariff Inn: Ireland—C-2384, G-2589, MCNY, AC

76. The Great Fight for the Championship Between John C. Heenan "The Benicia Boy" and Tom Sayers "Champion of England" Which took place April 17th 1860, at Farnborough, England—C-2613, G-2833, NYPL

77. Great Riot at the Astor Place Opera House, New York on Thursday Evening May 10th, 1849—C-2647, G-2868, LC, MCNY, NYHS

78. The Great Walk—Come in as you Can—C-2656, G-2875

79. The Great Walk—Come in as you can: The Finish—C-2654, G-2876 - LC, AC

80. The Great Walk—Go as you Please—C-2657, G-2877

81. The Great Walk—Go as you Please: The Start—C-2655 G-2878 LC, AC

82. His Eminence: Cardinal McCloskey—C-2834, G-3062, LC, MCNY

83. His Eminence Cardinal McCloskey: Born March 10, 1810; Died Oct. 10th, 1885—G-3063, MCNY

84. Holy Cross Abbey/on the Suir—C-2843, G-3074, MCNY, AC

85. The Holy Well: St. Fineen's Gougaune Barra, Ireland—C-2854, G-3087, LC, MCNY

86. Homeward Bound: (New York)—G-3120, MMA, AC

87. Hon. Charles Gavin Duffy: The Irish Patriot—C-2897, G-3131

88. Howth Castle: Dublin Bay—G-3210

89. Howth Castle: Ireland—C-2967, G-3211

90. Imposing the Cardinal's Beretta: Upon his Grace Archibishop McCloskey of New York, by his Grace Archbishop Bayley of Baltimore, at St. Patrick's Cathedral, N.Y. April 27th 1875—C-3043, G-3280, LC, MCNY

91. Innisfallen: Ireland—C-3115, G-3348

92. Innisfallen: Lake of Killarney, Ireland—G-3349

93. The Irish Beauty—C-3127, G-3367, CHS, LC, AC

94. James J. Corbett—Champion Heavyweight—C-3156, G-3404

95. James Stephens: Head Center of the Irish Republican Brotherhood—C-3174, G-3425

96. John C. Heenan "The Benicia Boy": Champion of the World—C-3263, G-3522, LC

97. John C. Heenan, The Champion of America: (The Benicia Boy)—C-3261, G-3523, LC

98. John C. Heenan, the Champion of America: ("The Benicia Boy")—C-3262, G-3524, LC

99. John C. Heenan, Champion of the World: ("The Benicia Boy")—C-3265, G-3525, CHS

100. John C. Heenan, Champion of the World: (The Benicia Boy)—C-3264, G-3526, NYPL, SI, AC

101. John Ennis: The Celebrated Pedestrian—C-3266, G-3527, LC, MCNY, AC

102. John J. Dwyer, Champion of America—C-3268, G-3531

103. John L. Sullivan: Champion Pugilist of the World—C-3270, G-3532, CHS, LC, AC

104. John Mitchel: The First Martyr of Ireland in Her Revolution of 1848 (Full Face Holding "United Irishman")—C-3272, G-3534, LC

105. John Mitchel: The First Martyr of Ireland in her Revolution of 1848 (Profile Holding "United Irishman")—C-3273, G-3535, LC, MCNY, AC

106. John Mitchel: The First Martyr of Ireland in Her Revolution of 1848 [vertical half-length portrait with facsimile signature]—C-3274, G-3536, MCNY

107. John Morrissey: Born February 5th, 1831, Height 6 Feet Weight 170 lbs.—C-3275, G-3537, LC

108. Kilkenny Castle: Ireland—C-3329, G-3594, LC, AC

109. The Killeries - Connemara—C-3330, G-3595, LC, AC

110. Killiney Hill: Near Dublin—C-3331, G-3596

111. King William III: Crossing the Boyne, July 1st 1690 [equestrian portrait]—G-3605, C-3341, MCNY

112. King William III: Crossing the Boyne July 1st 1690 [equestrian portrait]—G-3606, DIA, LC

113. King William III: Crossing the Boyne July 1st 1690 [equestrian portrait]—G-3607, MCNY PMA

114. King William III: Crossing the Boyne July 1st 1690 [full length equestrian portrait]—G-3608 PMA

115. King William III: Crossing the Boyne, July 1st 1690 [signature of artist on image]—C-3343, G-3609

116. King William III: Prince of Orange, Born November 4th 1650, Died March 8th 1701 [full-face portrait]—C-3344, G-3610

117. King William of Orange—C-3345, G-3611

118. The Lakes of Killarney—C-3422, G-3686, SI, AC

119. The Lakes of Killarney—C-3421, G-3687, LC, MCNY, AC

120. Lismore Castle: County Waterford—G-3828, MCNY, AC

121. Lismore Castle, County Waterford–C-3557, G-3829, LC, MCNY, AC
122. Londonderry, Ireland–C-3753, G-4067
123. Londonderry: Ireland–C-3754, G-4065
124. Londonderry: On the River Foyle, Ireland–C-3755, G-4066, AC
125. The Lower Lake of Killarney Kerry County, Ireland–C-3825, G-4147
126. Luggelaw County Wicklaw-Ireland–C-3839, G-4165, AC
127. The Magnificent O'Connell Funeral Car Passing the Park in New York City on Wednesday, September 22nd 1847–C-3877, G-4205, LC, MCNY, AC
128. The Man that Gave Barnum His Turn–C-3963, G-4300, RMA, AC
129. Le Marechal MacMahon Grand Commandant De L'Armee Francaise [included on list due to connection with Siege of Limerick]–G-4317
130. The Meeting of the Waters: In the Vale of Avoca, County Wicklow, Ireland–C-4102, G-4460, LC, AC
131. The Meeting of the Waters: In the Vale of Avoca, County Wicklow Ireland–C-4101, G-4461, LC MCNY, AC
132. Miniature Landscapes No. I: The Trout Stream; The Bridge Waterfall; Lighthouse Near Holyhead; Ben Venue, Scotland; Niagara Falls; Falls Near Tarrytown, N.Y.; The Giant's Causeway–C-4136, G-4499
133. The Most Rev. John Hughes, D.D.: First Archbishop of New York [bust portrait]–C-4224, G-4591, LC
134. The Most Rev. John Hughes, D.D.: First Archbishop of New York [three-quarter portrait]–C-4225, G-4592, LC, MCNY, AC
135. The Most Rev. John McCloskey D.D.: Second Archbishop of New York–C-4226, G-4593, CHS, GC, AC
136. Muckross Abbey, Killarney–C-4265, G-4633
137. My Pretty Irish Girl–C-4352, G-4727
138. The New St. Patrick's Cathedral Fifth Avenue, New York–C-4428, G-4812, NYPL
139. Nills Tower, Naworth–C-4479, G-4864
140. The O'Donoghue, MP: Ireland's Champion of Freedom–G-4923, NYPL
141. The Old Weir Bridge: Lakes of Killarney–C-4590, G-4975, AC
142. Orangemens Chart O.B.L.: Holiness to the Lord–C-4623, G-5009
143. O'Sullivan's Cascade: Lake of Killarney–C-4633, G-5022, MCNY, AC
144. "Ould Times" At Donnybrook Fair–C-4635, G-5025, MCNY, MMA, AC
145. Our Lady of Knock–C-4641, G-5033, GC, AC
146. Outward Bound (Dublin)–G-5059, MMA
147. Paddy and the Pigs–C-4689, G-5083, MCNY
148. Paddy Murphy's "Jantin Car"–C-4690, G-5084, MMA, AC

149. Paddy Ryan "The Trojan Giant"–C-4691, G-5085
150. A Pattern in Connemara: Ireland–C-4726, G-5124, MCNY
151. A Political Debate in the Darktown Club: Settling the Question–C-4821, G-5229, LC
152. A Political Debate in the Darktown Club: The Question Settled–C-4822, G-5230, LC
153. The Pride of Kildare–C-4913, G-5327, AC
154. The Propagation Society.–More Free Than Welcome–C-4962, G-5382, LC
155. Queenstown Harbor–C-5030, G-5446
156. Queenstown Harbor: Cove of Cork, Ireland–C-5031, G-5447
157. Rapids of Dunass: "On the Shannon"–C-5058, G-5484, MCNY, AC
158. Rathgallen Head: Scene in "The Shaughraun"–C-5067, G-5494, MCNY
159. The River Shannon From the Tower of Limerick Cathedral–C-5159, G-5595, MCNY
160. Robert Emmet/Dublin on the 19th Sept., 1803 [full-length courtroom scene]–C-5183
161. Robert Emmet/Dublin on the 19th of Sept. 1803 #725 [full-length courtroom scene surrounded by barristers]–C-5184, G-5620, PMA
162. Robert Emmet: Ireland's "Martyr of Freedom" [Lord Norbury on bench.]–C-5185, G-5622 PMA, AC
163. Robert Emmet: Ireland's "Martyr of Freedom"–C-5186 [full-length, additional line of quotation]
164. Robert Emmet's Betrothed–C-5187, G-5623
165. The Rose of Killarney–C-5211, G-5649, AC
166. The Rose of Killarney: Ballad by Miss Eliza Cook–C-5212, G-5650
167. Roserk Abbey–C-5218, G-5655
168. Ross Castle–Lake of Killarney–C-5221, G-5660, AC
169. Saint Bridget/Sta. Brigida–C-5311, G-5753, GC, NYHS
170. Saint Bridget: Sta. Brigida/Ste. Brigitte–G-5754, LC
171. Salmon Leap: River Shannon–C-5372, G-5760
172. Salmon Leap, near Ballyshannon, Ireland–C-5371, G-5761
173. A Scene in Old Ireland–C-5412, G-5808, LC, AC
174. Scenery of Connemara, Ireland: Ballinahinch Lake–C-5416, G-5812, MCNY
175. The Scenery of Ireland: Upper Lake of Killarney–C-5417, G-5813, LC
176. Scenery of Wicklow, Ireland: The Devils Glen–C-5420, G-5820, MCNY
177. The Seven Churches of Clonmacnoise: On the River Shannon, Ireland –C-5471, G-5871, PMA, AC
178. Shaughaun, Act II, Scene I–C-5485, G-5885, AC
179. The Siege of Limerick From the 9th to the 31st Aug 1690–C-5510, G-5908, MCNY
180. The Siege of Limerick from the 9th to the 31st of August 1690–C-5511, G-5909, LC, AC

181. Signal Fires on the Slievenamon Mountains: Ireland, 1848—C-5517, G-5912, LC, MCNY
182. Snap Apple Night All Hallow Eve—C-5576, G-5971 MCNY
183. A Stag Hunt at Killarney—C-5690, G-6095
184. St. Bridget, Abbess of Kildare—C-5310, G-6126
185. St. Fineen's Well, Ireland—C-5322, G-6234, LC
186. St. Patrick/San Patrico [half length holding a crosier]—C-5352, G-6286, LC
187. St. Patrick/St. Patricio [same with slight differences]—C-5351, G-6287, GC
188. St. Patrick The Apostle of Ireland: Born in the Year 361—Died in the year 458 [full-length with reptiles at his feet]—C-5353, G-6288, GC
189. St. Patrick the Apostle of Ireland: Born in the Year 361, died in the year 458—G-6289
190. Thomas F. Meagher [three-quarter length standing with hand on chair]—C-6023, G-6495, LC
191. Thomas F. Meagher Ireland 1848 [seated, profile with boat scene through window]—C-6024, G-6496, LC
192. Thomas Francis Meagher [in uniform, left hand holding sword and right hand holds a cap]—C-6025, G-6497, MCNY
193. Trial of the Irish Patriots at Clonmel, Oct. 22nd 1848 Thos. F. Meagher, Terence B. McManus, Patrick O'Donohue, Receiving their Sentence—C-6147, G-6631, LC
194. The Upper Lake of Killarney: Kerry County, Ireland—C-6353, G-6807
195. The Valley of the Blackwater: Scenery of Ireland—C-6356, G-6865, MCNY, AC
196. The Very Reverend Father Theobold Matthew—C-6370, G-6877
197. The Very Reverend Theobold Matthew: This print is respectfully dedicated to the members of the temperance societies, throughout the world—C-6369, G-6870, LC
198. Very Rev. Father Thos. N. Burke, O. P. The Champion of Irish History—C-6368, G-6879, LC, AC
199. Wearing of the Green—C-6594, G-7117
200. Wicklow, Ireland—C-6656, G-7198
201. Wm. Smith O'Brien: Ireland's Patriot 1848—C-6704, G-7297, LC, AC
202. The Yacht "Dauntless" of New York: Off Queenstown Ireland July 13th 1869—C-6796, G-7351, LC
203. Yankee Doodle on his Muscle: Or the Way the Benecia Boy Astonished the English Men—C-6822, G-7377, LC, MCNY, NYPL, AC

Note: Print on page 52 Courtesy of the Eno Collection. Miriam and Ira D. Wallach Division of Art, Prints and Photographs. The New York Public Library. Astor, Lenox and Tilden Foundations

SELECT BIBLIOGRAPHY

BOOKS

Anderson, Bern. *By Sea and By River, The Naval History of the Civil War.*
Westport, Conn: Greenwood Press, 1977.

Boucicault, Dion. *The Shaughraun.*
New York: Samuel French Publishers, 1925.

Boylan, Henry. *Wolf Tone.*
Dublin: Gill and Macmillan Ltd., 1981.

Boylan, Henry. *A Valley of Kings: The Boyne.*
Dublin: The O'Brien Press Ltd., 1988.

Bradley, Kathleen. *History of the Irish in America.*
Seacaucus, N.J.: Chartwell Books Division of Book Sales, Inc., 1986.

Callaghan, Mary Rose. *Kitty O'Shea, Life of Katherine Parnell.*
London: Pandora Press, Unwin Hyman Ltd., 1989.

Carthy, Margaret. *A Cathedral of Suitable Magnificence.*
Wilmington, Del.: Michael Glazier, Inc., 1984.

Cavanagh, Michael. *Memoirs of Gen. Thomas Francis Meagher.*
Worcester, Mass.: Messenger Press, 1892.

Conningham, Frederick A. *Currier and Ives Prints An Illustrated Check List.*
New York: Crown Publishers Inc., 1983.

Davis, Burke, and Roy King. *The World of Currier and Ives.*
New York: Bonanza Books, 1987.

deBreffny, Brian. *Castles of Ireland.*
London: Thames and Hudson Ltd., 1977.

Devoy, John. *The Land of Eire, Its Struggles, Prospects, Scenery and Antiquities.*
New York: Patterson and Neilson, 1882.

Dibble, R. F. *John L. Sullivan.*
Boston: Little, Brown, and Co., 1925.

Dillon, William. *The Life of John Mitchel.* 2 Vols.
London: Kegan, Paul, Trench and Co., 1888.

Ellis, Peter Berresford. *The Boyne Water.*
Belfast: The Blackstaff Press Ltd., 1989.

Gale Research Company. *Currier and Ives, A Catalogue Raisonne.*
Detroit: Gale Research Company, 1984.

Golding, Louis. *The Bare-Knuckle Breed.*
London: Hutchinson and Co., Ltd., 1952.

Gorn, Elliott, J. *The Manly Art.*
Ithaca, New York: Cornell University Press, 1986

Griffith, Arthur. *Meagher of the Sword.*
Dublin: M. H. Gill and Son, Ltd., 1916.

Hayward, Richard. *Where the River Shannon Flows.*
Dundalk, Ireland: Dundalgan Press, 1950.

Inglis, Brian. *The Story of Ireland.*
London: Faber and Faber, 1956.

The Irish Question.
St. Paul, Minn.: Greenhaven Press, Inc., 1979.

Jennett, Sean. *Munster.*
London: Faber & Faber Ltd., 1967.

Johnson, James E. *The Irish In America.*
Minneapolis, Minn.: Lerner Publications Company, 1966.

Jones, Paul. *The Irish Brigade.*
Washington and New York: Robert B. Luce, Inc., 1969

Joyce, James. *A Portrait of the Artist as a Young Man.*
New York: Viking Penguin, 1977.

Joyce, T. W. *Atlas and Encyclopedia of Ireland:* Part I, *A Comprehensive Delineation of the Thirty-two Counties.*
New York: Murphy and McCarthy, 1902.

Kilroy, Patricia. *The Story of Connemara.*
Dublin: Gill and Macmillan, Ltd., 1989.

MacDonald, John. *Great Battlefields of the World.*
New York: Macmillan Publishing Company, 1985.

McCallum, John D. *The World Heavyweight Championship, A History.*
Radnor, PA: Chilton Book Company, 1974.

McClain, Craig. *Currier and Ives an Illustrated Value Guide.*
Lombard, Ill.: Wallace-Hemstead Book Co., 1987

McGee, Col. James E. *The Men of '48.*
New York: J. A. McGee, l874.

MacManus, Seamus. *The Story of the Irish Race.*
New York: Devin-Adair, 1944.

Mitchel, John. *Jail Journal.*
Glasgow: Cameron, Ferguson and Co.(Author's Edition)

O'Duigneain, Proinnsios. *North Leitrim : The Land War and the Fall of Parnell.*
Nure, Ireland: Proinnsios O'Duigneain, n.d.

O'Hanlon, Rev. John Canon. *Irish-American History of the United States.*
New York: Murphy and Son, 1907.

Parnell, John Howard. *Charles Stuart Parnell, A Memoir.*
New York: Henry Holt & Co., 1914.

Peters, Harry T. *Currier & Ives, Printmakers to the American People.*
Garden City, N.Y.: Doubleday, Doran & Co., Inc., 1942.

Ranelagh, John. *Ireland, An Illustrated History.*
New York: Oxford University Press, 1981.

Rawls, Walton. *The Great Book of Currier & Ives America.*
New York: Abbeville Press, 1979.

Ryan, Desmond. *The Fenian Chief.*
Dublin: M. H. Gill & Son, Ltd., 1967.

Ryan, Dr. Mark F. *Fenian Memories.*
Dublin: M. H. Gill & Son, Ltd., 1946.

Sammons, Jeffrey T. *Beyond the Ring.*
Urbana and Chicago: University of Illinois Press, 1988.

Scherman, Katharine. *The Flowering of Ireland, Saints, Scholars and Kings.*
Boston: Little, Brown and Co., 1981.

Schurre, Jacques. *Currier and Ives Prints, A Checklist of Unrecorded Prints.*
New York: Personal publication, 1984

Shields, Hugh, ed. *Old Dublin Songs.*
Dublin: Folk Music Society of Ireland, 1988.

Simkin, Colin. *Currier and Ives America.*
New York: Crown Publishers Inc., 1952.

Sullivan, John, with Abbe Mac-Goeghegan and John Mitchel.*The History of Ireland, Ancient and Modern.*
New York: D. and J. Sadlier & Co., 1869.

Touhill, Blanche M. *William Smith O'Brien and His Irish Revolutionary Companions in Penal Exile.*
Columbia: University of Missouri Press, 1981.

Trench, Charles Chenevix. *The Great Dan.*
London: Triad Grafton Books, 1986.

Wallace, Martin. *A Short History of Ireland.*
Belfast: Appletree Press Ltd., 1986.

Walsh, Townsend. *The Career of Dion Boucicault.*
New York: The Dunlop Society, 1915.

ARTICLES AND PAMPHLETS

Anon. "John Morrissey." *Harper's Weekly,* May 18, 1878, 389.

Anon. "Thomas Francis Meagher." *Harper's Weekly,* July 27, 1867, 478.

Anon. "Welcome to Saint Patrick's Cathedral."
New York: Saint Patrick's Cathedral Parish House, n.d.

Magriel, Paul. "A Note on John L. Sullivan."
New York: Reporter Publications, Inc. *Gentry volume #2,* 1952.

Murphy, William A. *Origins of the Fenian Movement in New York.* Unpublished academic paper.

Wilshin, Francis F. "Manassas."
Washington, D.C.: National Park Service Historial Handbook. Series Number 15, reprint, 1961

Witnes, I. "The Champion."
New York: Reporter Publications, Inc., *Gentry volume #2,* 1952.

INDEX